LONDON MIDLAND STEAM

1948-1966

BEN BROOKSBANK
PETER TUFFREY

GREAT N ORTHERN

ACKNOWLEDGEMENTS

We would like to thank the following people for their help: Rosemary Brooksbank, David Burrill, Peter Crangle, D.J. Dippie, Peter Jary, Hugh Parkin.

Special thanks are due to Peter Tuffrey's son Tristram for his help and encouragement throughout the project.

INFORMATION

We have taken reasonable steps to verify the accuracy of the information in this book but it may contain errors or omissions. Any information that may be of assistance to rectify any problems will be gratefully received. Please contact by email petertuffrey@rocketmail.com or in writing to Peter Tuffrey, 8 Wrightson Avenue, Warmsworth, Doncaster, South Yorkshire, DN4 9QL.

Great Northern Books
PO Box 1380, Bradford, BD5 5FB
www.greatnorthernbooks.co.uk

Every effort has been made to acknowledge correctly and contact the copyright holders of material in this book. Great Northern Books Ltd apologises for any unintentional errors or omissions, which should be notified to the publisher.

ISBN: 978-1-912101-92-4

Design and layout: David Burrill

CIP Data
A catalogue for this book is available from the British Library

Printed & bound in India

INTRODUCTION

Throughout B.W.L. 'Ben' Brooksbank's life his passion has been the railways. This has been manifested in several publications on railway history and many thousands of photographs — of both locomotives and stations — taken across the country from 1946-1968. Here, a selection of Ben's images of the London Midland Region of British Railways have been assembled and cover the period 1948-1966.

This area originated from the London Midland & Scottish Railway, which was the largest railway company created by the Grouping of 1923. The company weathered the challenging financial climate of the 1920s and 1930s through to the outbreak of war in 1939. The 'Big Four' railways then came under Government control for the duration and in the years immediately after victory.

After six long years of gruelling conflict, the British people wanted to improve their standard of living and favoured a Labour government to help them achieve this. Sweeping to power in 1945, the party had grand plans for the rebirth of the nation and these were centred on nationalised industries and a National Health Service. The railways were dealt with in the Transport Act 1947 which sought to integrate the many modes of transport to increase efficiency and stabilise employment.

The newly formed British Railways was organised in 1948 into Regions — Eastern, London Midland, North Eastern, Scottish, Southern and Western — taking as a guide the boundaries of the 'Big Four' companies, the notable exception being Scotland, which was unified. The London Midland Region encompassed much of the LMSR lines in England: the West Coast Main Line from Euston to Carlisle; Midland main line from St Pancras to Carlisle; routes to Liverpool and Manchester; the mining areas of the Midlands; the industrial north west; branch lines; commuter routes around major cities, such as London, Birmingham, etc.

There was some overlap between the Regions, as there always had been, with companies jostling for the mineral and industrial wealth of various areas. In the east, the LMR had access to Peterborough, which was a stronghold of the Eastern Region, for the transfer of freight and passengers. Similarly, in the west the LMR encroached on the Western Region, running services to Shrewsbury, along the North Wales Coast Line to Holyhead and through to Bristol, although the LMR boundary was in the Ashchurch area.

In 1948, the LMR also had lines in the West Riding of Yorkshire (now West and South Yorkshire), but in 1958 these were transferred to the Eastern and North Eastern Regions, whilst the ex-GCR 'London' Extension was given to the LMR. The Western Region also received responsibility for the notorious Lickey Incline and the ex-LMSR 0-6-0T locomotives were replaced by the ex-GWR 94XX Class.

The LMR inherited nearly 8,000 locomotives in 1948 and these were quite diverse. The Midland Railway 0-6-0s of Johnson design were still employed on local freight and mineral trains on and around the Midland main line, as were the LNWR 0-8-0s. There was also a relatively small number of ex-Lancashire & Yorkshire Railway locomotives still in existence.

The LMSR — under CMEs Sir Henry Fowler and W.A. Stanier — adopted a policy of standardisation to improve maintenance and reliability, which was lacking in many old LNWR and MR locomotives. George Hughes (CME from 1923 to 1925) produced the first standard class for the company — a mixed traffic 2-6-0 which eventually numbered some 245 examples. Fowler followed this lead by adapting his MR 3835 Class 0-6-0 design and the 4F Standard Goods Class became a familiar sight across the country. In the late 1920s the 'Royal Scot' express passenger locomotives were introduced and followed by the 'Patriot' Class 4-6-0s.

Despite the infusion of new motive power, the stock of the LMSR was not very modern or reliable. Stanier's appointment in the early 1930s was an attempt to rectify this and the company supported him with major orders for several new classes. He began by integrating his ideas into the Hughes 2-6-0 and 40 new engines were constructed in 1933/1934. Stanier was then able to refine the designs for major new classes — 'Princess Royal' Pacific; 'Jubilee' 4-6-0; Class 5 4-6-0; 8F 2-8-0. After initial problems with the superheater had been corrected (too few elements were used), the 4-6-0s became useful and reliable classes, whilst the Pacific developed further into the 'Coronation' Class, which would be the mainstay of the WCML expresses until the end of steam. The robust 8F freight engines were chosen by the REC during the war as a Standard Design, also influencing the WD 'Austerity' Class 2-8-0s that would work on the LMSR after the war.

The LMR had a solid group of engines in the late 1940s, but additions were still necessary to replace life-expired classes that had survived due to the war. Former LMSR employee — and pupil of Stanier — R.A. Riddles was appointed as Mechanical and Electrical Engineer for British Railways and was influenced by LMSR designs for the new Standard Classes. The vast majority of these types would work for various periods on the LMR, becoming just as recognisable as the older classes.

B.W.L. 'Ben' Brooksbank was born shortly after Grouping and matured a short distance away from the Birmingham-Gloucester-Bristol-Birmingham line, which was operated by the LMSR. As with many boys from the period, he became fascinated with the railway, particularly the old MR engines and the new Stanier locomotives working the many passenger and freight trains through the area. Ben was 'incarcerated' at boarding school in his early teens, but he benefitted from having to travel there by rail, which opened his interest into the 'scene' further afield; he also had relatives in Liverpool and holidayed around the country during the war, improving his familiarity with the wider network.

During his leisure time Ben spent many hours 'train-watching' at Ashchurch, Gloucester, Worcester and in London. This coincided with the Second World War, meaning there was plenty of traffic to see and record. Of this latter activity, Ben comments that he has notebooks filled with locomotive numbers accompanied by meticulous details of the workings — a practice that continued to the end of steam; Ben suggests he has perhaps seen the vast majority of the locomotives inherited by BR at Nationalisation. However, taking notes during the war was not without risk and in 1945 a 'spy-catching' passenger reported Ben to the railway police at York station, but a sensible officer just gave the young man a warning.

Ben's first camera (a 'Box Brownie') was received as a Christmas present in 1945 and from then on he took as many pictures as he could of the railways. The availability of film was a stumbling block at first and reels of surplus RAF stock had to be acquired; the process of developing the prized pictures was entrusted to local shops, with decidedly mixed results. He upgraded to a second hand Kodak Retina in late 1947 to improve the quality and used this until the camera disintegrated through overuse in 1956. Various SLR cameras were then employed through to the end of steam, when the 'wretched' diesels finally took over.

In 1948 Ben entered full-time employment as an academic scientist (earning £300 p.a.), but he still found time to 'train-watch' and used his spare income to travel across the country (by rail to 1955 — at least 5,000 miles a year) recording the various locomotives and their workings through to 1968. He also joined the Railway Correspondence and Travel Society, which allowed visits to various sheds and works, which would have otherwise been inaccessible. Ben observes that he preferred to photograph locomotives in stations, as he was interested in the latter as well (incredibly, Ben has taken a picture of every station in Britain with a name beginning with the letter 'B').

Not focussing on any particular area, Ben took many interesting pictures all over the LMR between 1948 and 1966, capturing the various locomotive types at work and rest, as well as stations and lines long since disappeared. Examples include: part of the line between Derby and Manchester; the 'London Extension'; the Nottingham-Worksop route; Manchester Exchange station; Nottingham Victoria; Tebay station. Similarly, the locomotive sheds — once an exotic place enthusiasts would dream of conquering, but more importantly a place of employment for many — have all been closed, which gives a good indication of the complete change instigated by the arrival of diesels.

The LMR's motive power is well-represented in this book, ranging from the old Midland and LNWR engines ready for withdrawal in the late 1940s, the ex-MR Johnson 0-6-0s which would survive a little longer, the Fowler classes quietly going about their business, the Stanier Class 5 and 8Fs covered in grime, but still efficient, while a bit of 'glamour' is provided by (some) neatly turned out named 'Jubilee' 4-6-0s and 'Coronation' Pacifics. The next generation of locomotives — the BR Standards — also appear, with the 'Britannia' Pacifics included along with Class 5 4-6-0s, Class 4 4-6-0s, Class 4 2-6-0s, Class 3 2-6-2Ts and the heavy freight 9F 2-10-0s.

Unfortunately, all of these had a very short lifespan due to the Modernisation Plan. Some of the schemes set out by this are captured in these pages: the WCML electrification at several sites; rebuilding of stations at Weaver Junction, Manchester London Road (later Piccadilly) and Tamworth.

Thankfully, the introduction of diesels did not mean the end of interest in steam locomotives. Ben — now 91 — still has the same enthusiasm for them as he did all those years ago and offers this selection for your enjoyment.

Above **ACTON BRIDGE**

Stanier 'Jubilee' Class 4-6-0 no. 45599 *Bechuanaland* steams south towards Acton Bridge on the West Coast Main Line in early August 1962. The engine is at the head of a Class C freight train, formed from three Type A containers and an assortment of vans.

Below **ACTON BRIDGE STATION**

View north at Acton Bridge station as Stanier 8F Class no. 48260 passes through with a freight on 23rd December 1961. The engine was based at Birkenhead and would remain there until June 1965.

Above ALFRETON & SOUTH NORMANTON STATION

BR Standard Class 4 no. 75062 passes through Alfreton & South Normanton station with an Up parcels train on 23rd June 1961. The station opened as Alfreton but had the second portion added from November 1891 and remained in use until closure on 2nd January 1967; the station has since reopened.

Opposite above ACTON BRIDGE

Built at Swindon Works in July 1944, Stanier 8F Class 2-8-0 no. 48448 was employed by the Great Western Railway until May 1947, when returned to the LMSR. Before the end of the decade the engine was allocated to Birkenhead shed and remained there until mid-1965, when transferred to Burnley Rose Grove depot. Here, (18th September 1965) no. 48448 travels south with a freight at Acton Bridge on the WCML. The engine was condemned in July 1968.

Opposite below ALFRETON & SOUTH NORMANTON STATION

The North Midland Railway and Eastern Counties Railway both missed the important industrial areas of the Erewash Valley when they were constructed in the late 1830s. After formation in the mid-1840s, the Midland Railway set about rectifying this and a line from Long Eaton to Pinxton was soon completed, but the remainder to connect with the NMR section from Derby to Chesterfield was not laid until 1862. On this part was Alfreton & South Normanton station, where 8F no. 48176 is seen heading a train of empty coal wagons north on 23rd June 1961; in the distance is Coates Park Colliery spoil heap.

Above AMPTHILL STATION

Ampthill station — on the Midland main line between Bedford and Luton — was closed in May 1959 after just over 90 years serving local travellers to and from the area. A year following closure (on 30th April 1960), Johnson 3F Class 0-6-0 no. 43474 passes through the station remains with a short Down freight train.

Opposite above AMERSHAM STATION

Until 1958 Amersham station was under the jurisdiction of the Eastern Region, being on the ex-Metropolitan & Great Central Railway section of the GCR's London Extension. During the BR period several boundary changes occurred but the most comprehensive took place in 1958 and the entire GCR main line handed over to the London Midland Region in return for much of the latter's lines in Yorkshire. A greater proportion of LMR locomotives were then to be seen on the GCR route, one being Stanier Class 5 4-6-0 no. 45215. This engine was transferred to Leicester GCR shed following the change of management and had recently been sent to Neasden to work from the London end of the line. No. 45215 is seen here on 19th May 1959 heading north with the 13.30 stopping train from Marylebone.

Opposite below APSLEY STATION

BR Standard Class 7 Pacific no. 70044 approaches Apsley station (just north of Watford) with a Down express on 18th July 1953. Only a month earlier the engine had been completed at Crewe Works and had evidently not reached Norwich, which was no. 70044's first allocation. Both nos 70043 and 70044 were fitted when new with Westinghouse air brakes (seen here mounted on both sides of the smokebox) as part of trials then being conducted by BR into the merits of this type and the vacuum method then in widespread use.

Above ASHCHURCH STATION

The Birmingham-Bristol route was established early in the history of the railways due to the importance of transporting goods from inland to the port at Bristol. The Birmingham & Gloucester Railway constructed that section of the route in 1840, whilst the Bristol & Gloucester Railway completed the other in 1844, both later joined to become the Birmingham & Bristol Railway. Shortly after the MR bought the whole line, which later passed to the London, Midland & Scottish Railway and part of which — as far as Ashchurch —was inherited by the LMR at Nationalisation. Fowler 4F Class 0-6-0 no. 43951 is seen at Ashchurch rushing south with a coal train on 25th May 1957.

Opposite above ASHCHURCH STATION

Instead of idling away the last Saturday of May 1957 'spotting' locomotives in various places around Birmingham, youths affiliated with The Life Boys — the junior branch of the Boys' Brigade — have been whisked away to the West Country for more gainful endeavours. One of Bushbury's Stanier 'Jubilee' 4-6-0s (no. 45688 *Polyphemus*) has been finely fettled for the occasion and is seen transporting the party south at the north end of Ashchurch station.

Opposite below ASHCHURCH STATION

Ashchurch was the meeting place for the southern ends of two ex-MR loop lines; Evesham to the east and Great Malvern to the west. On the latter was Tewkesbury and where Ivatt Class 2 2-6-0 no. 46401 was destined for with the carriage in the branch platform on the right. The engine was based at the MR's former shed in Gloucester and had three years there from 1956 to 1959.

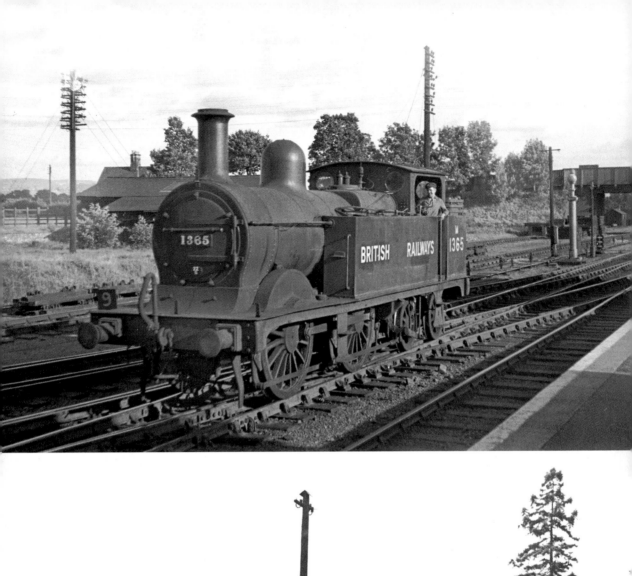

Above **ASHCHURCH STATION**

View north to Ashchurch station from the main road between Tewkesbury and Toddington (formerly the A438, now A46 from the M5 to Coventry via Evesham, Alcester and Warwick). The Evesham loop curves away on the right — with an ex-GWR 2-8-0 waiting for the main line — and the Tewkesbury branch is on the left. Passing through the middle on 25th May 1957 is Class 5 4-6-0 no. 45056 with the 08.06 from Sheffield to Gloucester. A new signal box is in the midst of construction, but this only lasted for just over ten years following opening in 1958. Ashchurch station was a casualty in the early 1970s, only to be resurrected in 1997.

Opposite above **ASHCHURCH STATION**

MR Johnson/Deeley 0-4-4T no. 1365 was engaged on no. 9 pilot duty at Ashchurch station when captured in this picture from 29th July 1949. Constructed by Dübs & Co. in May 1882, the engine amassed an impressive 69 years in service. The locomotive was due to take no. 58063 but was condemned before this change could take place, although no. 1365 has the rare 'M' prefix applied briefly after Nationalisation in 1948.

Opposite below **ASHCHURCH STATION**

Fowler 4P Class 2-6-4T no. 42337 pauses at Ashchurch with the 09.41 train to Birmingham New Street station via Evesham on 8th August 1959. The line between Birmingham and Gloucester bypassed several communities to the east when laid. In the late 1850s the MR decided to serve these, beginning with a line running from Barnt Green to Redditch, then Ashchurch to Evesham in 1864. The final sections from Evesham to Alcester and from there to Redditch being ready in 1866 and 1868 respectively. Despite the importance of this route for avoiding the notorious Lickey Incline on the main line, the condition of the track was allowed to deteriorate and, following a partial closure in the early 1960s, the whole line was closed in 1964.

Above **ATHERSTONE**

Hughes 'Crab' Class 2-6-0 no. 42811 was the second of forty locomotives built to the design at Horwich Works between April 1929 and December 1930. As LMSR no. 13111 the engine started work at Aston, Birmingham, before moving north to Liverpool Edge Hill. Returning to the aforementioned depot in the early 1930s, by the middle of the decade (when the engine was renumbered 2811) a move to Warrington had occurred and the locomotive spent the remainder of the 1930s and the war years working in and around Manchester and Liverpool. No. 42811 was employed at Crewe South shed for the majority of the 1950s and, after several moves to depots on the WCML in 1960, had 18 months at Nuneaton until withdrawn from Chester after only a month there in July 1962. The locomotive is seen here just north of Nuneaton at Atherstone with a Class E freight on 28th December 1961.

Above **ATTENBOROUGH STATION**

View from the footbridge at the south-west end of Attenborough station as Stanier 8F 2-8-0 no. 48362 heads towards Nottingham with a freight train on 23rd June 1961. The station was a late addition to the line between Derby and Nottingham, only opening for passengers in 1856 and lasting until 1858. Six years later a second station was built and this has remained in use ever since, although much altered with the brick supports for the footbridge the only original features remaining, the rest has been demolished and replaced. No. 48362 was erected at Horwich Works in August 1944 and subsequently had two spells working from Toton, which was a short distance away to the west, from at least Nationalisation to June 1962 when loaned briefly to Nottingham. Returning until April 1964 no. 48362 moved on to Wellingborough and continued in service until December 1967, being withdrawn from Edge Hill shed.

Above **BAKEWELL**

BR Standard Class 5 4-6-0 no. 73143 works hard up the difficult incline of 1 in 100 from Rowsley to Peak Forest (15 miles) on the ex-MR line from the main route north of Derby to Manchester. The locomotive is seen north of Bakewell and is attached to a fully-laden coal train, which has a banker assisting at the rear (but unseen here), on 23rd June 1961.

Opposite above **BAGILLT STATION**

Stanier Class 5 no. 45256 arrives at Bagillt station with the 11.10 stopping train from Llandudno for Chester on 7th September 1962. The photograph also shows the Point of Ayr and the Dee Estuary which the Holyhead to Chester line parallelled for a number for a number of miles.

Opposite below **BAGULEY**

A train of empty coal wagons is hauled eastward at Baguley, Wythenshawe, on the ex-Cheshire Lines Committee route to Stockport, in early May 1965. At the head is Class 5 no. 45059 of Speke Junction shed; the engine worked there for the final two years in service, being condemned in July 1967.

Above **BAKEWELL STATION**

Fowler's 4F Class 0-6-0 was a development of his earlier MR 3835 Class. After Grouping, the design was chosen to be the LMSR's standard goods engine and the vast majority of the 575 class total were erected between 1923 and 1928; 45 were completed in the late 1930s and early 1940s. No. 44172 entered service from Crewe Works in March 1926 and was subsequently a long-term resident at Rowsley shed. The engine had perhaps been engaged from there as a banker when pictured on the southbound platform at Bakewell station on 23rd June 1961.

Opposite above **BARNT GREEN STATION**

An express freight heads north through Barnt Green station on the Birmingham-Gloucester line, 16th August 1963. The station was opened in 1844 and saw several changes subsequently. The first occurred with the completion of the first stage of the Evesham loop in the late 1850s as the platforms were staggered to allow interchange between the two lines. Another platform was provided on the branch before the turn of the century, but after some 30 years another rebuilding took place and the main line platforms were resited adjacent to each other. Latterly, the station buildings have been completely removed but waiting shelters are currently provided. Fowler 4F no. 44226 had a long association with Saltley shed and was almost a year away from being withdrawn from there.

Opposite below **BARROW UPON SOAR STATION**

Ex-LNWR 0-8-0 no. 49450 heads a Toton-Willesden freight on 6th October 1950 through Barrow upon Soar station.

Above BELL BUSK

In the wilds of North Yorkshire and Cumbria (where the MR's Settle to Carlisle line ran), extremes in the weather — principally snow in the winter months — were a threat to the flow of railway traffic. Stanier 8F no. 48157 has been equipped with a snow plough to combat this problem, which was perhaps still a concern given the date the picture was taken — 21st April 1961. Despite looking slightly damp the weather is fine enough for the engine to head south unhindered through Bell Busk with a mixed freight train.

Opposite above BEIGHTON

The village of Beighton, south east of Sheffield, was the meeting place for the MR and GCR main lines; the latter crosses over the former by the second bridge on the left in the distance. The immediate area was also industrially important resulting in frequent traffic. WD 'Austerity' Class 2-8-0 no. 90649 has collected a train of loaded coal wagons from one of the pits and travels south on 13th July 1963.

Opposite below BESCOT JUNCTION

A local service between Birmingham New Street station and Walsall leaves the main line at Bescot Junction on 24th March 1951. Fowler 4P Class 2-6-2T no. 40066, which was allocated to Bushbury at this time, is at the head of the train. On the right in the distance is Bescot No. 3 signal box and beyond that was the engine shed and marshalling yard. This location is presently dominated by the M6 motorway which passes above the railway.

Above **BOURNEVILLE SHED**

Bourneville shed was established quite late in 1895 to the south of the station of the same name. Generally, the allocation was quite small and in 1946 there were only 28 locomotives on the roster, mainly being 0-6-0s but also including 4-4-0s, 2-6-4T, 2-6-2T and 0-6-0T types. Several of the 0-6-0s were used on the Halesowen branch, one being no. 22846 which is seen at the shed on 27th July 1947. The locomotive had been built to Kirtley's 700 Class design in the early 1870s and survived until October 1949.

Opposite above **BESCOT SHED**

Being close to a major marshalling yard, Bescot shed always had a large number of goods locomotives on hand. One of the types that was always in evidence was the Bowen Cooke G1 and G2A Class and Beames G2 Class 0-8-0s. Two, no. 49126 (G2A, right) and 49430 (G2, left), are seen here on 4th September 1962 hidden by two large coal stacks. The first mentioned engine had just been withdrawn from service, but the latter would return to be the last G2 withdrawn from service in December 1964.

Opposite below **BIRKENHEAD SHED**

Stanier 8F Class 2-8-0 no. 48660 has a crisis of identities. Despite having the new BR number on the smokebox door and the cab-side, 'LMS' is still on the tender — even though the company had been defunct six months when this picture was taken at Birkenhead shed. The locomotive had been constructed for the LMSR by the Southern Railway at Eastleigh in November 1943 and was subsequently allocated to Willesden shed (being noted there at Nationalisation and carrying the 1A shedcode here) but was later transferred to Birkenhead before spells at Swansea, Shrewsbury and Bath.

Above **BROMFORD BRIDGE RACECOURSE STATION**

The Birmingham & Derby Junction Railway was promoted in the mid-1830s to run from Derby via Burton and Tamworth to Hampton-in-Arden where a connection was to be formed with the London & Birmingham Railway. The project was soon taken up and completed in mid-1839. However, the use of the latter company's route proved too costly and the B&DJR resolved to build their own route into Birmingham, making a new junction at Water Orton and proceeding into the city via Castle Bromwich and Saltley to a terminus at Lawley Street. This was completed in early 1842 and a small station called Bromford Forge opened a few months later on this section, but closure followed swiftly. Before the end of the 19th century a racecourse opened nearby and to cash in on the excursion traffic the MR opened a new station on the site called Bromford Bridge Racecourse. However, this was only for said traffic and was only open for meetings. Stanier Class 5 no. 45668 passes the platforms with a mineral train on 5th September 1962.

Opposite above **BIRMINGHAM NEW STREET STATION**

At Birmingham New Street station on 14th April 1949, Thompson B1 no. 61325 comes off the 06.52 from Cleethorpes via Nottingham, whilst Hughes 'Crab' no. 2758 waits to leave with a train to Bristol.

Opposite below **BIRMINGHAM NEW STREET STATION**

Stanier 'Jubilee' Class no. 45709 *Implacable* stands at New Street's platform three on 11th August 1956 with the 13.55 Wolverhampton to London Euston service.

Above BLACKWELL STATION

The difficult two-mile Lickey incline (1 in 37.7 from Bromsgrove to Blackwell) has been completed by Stanier Class 5 no. 44962 which is in charge of the 09.05 Paignton to Birmingham relief service on 18th August 1960.

Opposite above BIRMINGHAM NEW STREET STATION

Birmingham Curzon Street station's usefulness had dwindled by the time the London & North Western Railway was formed in 1846 and the new company began the process of building a new station closer to the centre of the city near New Street. The opening occurred on 1st June 1854, with the MR also making use of the facilities. Space proved insufficient for both companies and by the end of the 1870s the situation required action. On the south side of New Street station a large train shed with four through platforms was constructed and in operation by 1885. Ivatt Class 4MT no. 43049 rests on the through road between platforms six and seven in this section of New Street station on 30th October 1959.

Opposite below BIRMINGHAM SALTLEY STATION

A short distance north of the original Birmingham Lawley Street terminus of the line from Derby was Saltley station which opened on 1st October 1854. Originally there were two island platforms but there was just one following reconstruction for widening works at the turn of the century. The north end is the location for this photograph (taken 22nd April 1965) as Fowler 4F Class no. 44057 runs northward tender first on the Up Camp Hill goods line. The locomotive could be heading to Washwood Heath sidings, which were in this direction, after being serviced at Saltley shed — located just to the south east. No. 44057 was allocated across Birmingham at Bescot but would spend five months at Saltley before withdrawal in November 1965. Saltley station was closed on 4th March 1968 and the site cleared.

Above **BLETCHLEY STATION**

Stanier 'Coronation' Class Pacific no. 46234 *Duchess of Abercorn* makes an unscheduled stop at Bletchley station to take on water. Working an Up service on 22nd December 1956, the locomotive has perhaps been unable to collect from Castlethorpe water troughs due to another express taking the supply and the process of refilling had not been completed; the tender's water scoop could also have been broken. No. 46234 was working from Crewe North and would remain there until November 1959 when transferred to Carlisle Upperby.

Opposite above **BLETCHLEY**

Just north of Bletchley (near Denbigh Hall signal box) Fowler rebuilt 'Royal Scot' Class 4-6-0 no. 46122 *Royal Ulster Rifleman* conveys Manchester United supporters to Wembley for the FA Cup Final on 4th May 1957. Aston Villa took on the 'Busby Babes' and triumphed 2-1, although United were down to ten men for much of the tie due to an injury to the goalkeeper.

Opposite below **BLETCHLEY STATION**

On 24th May 1958 'Coronation' Class Pacific no. 46239 *City of Chester* was rostered to the 08.00 Blackpool Central to London Euston express and the train is seen here at Bletchley station. The locomotive was erected at Crewe Works in August 1939 and spent many years allocated to Camden shed.

Above **BOLTON TRINITY STREET STATION**

'Crab' Class no. 42727 passes through Bolton Trinity Street station with a mineral train on 20th August 1963.

Below **BOLTON TRINITY STREET STATION**

The 16.52 Bolton Trinity Street to Stockport stands at the Up platform behind Stanier 4MT 2-6-4T no. 42647 before starting the journey on 3rd May 1965.

Above **BRADFORD FORSTER SQAURE STATION**

After inheriting the Leeds & Bradford Railway's station in Bradford, the MR was obliged to build a new station, not once but twice. The second, which was completed in 1890 to the design of Charles Trubshaw, is seen here on 22nd April 1961 looking south. There were six platforms under an overall glazed roof but this latter has unfortunately been lost by this time; the entire station has subsequently been demolished and replaced by a smaller facility on the west side (right here) of the site.

Below **BRADFORD LOW MOOR SHED**

Lancashire & Yorkshire Railway Hughes Class 6 2-6-2T no. 10952 at Bradford Low Moor shed on 25th May 1947; withdrawal would occur by June 1948.

Above **BRADWELL STATION**

Ivatt Class 3MT 2-6-2T no. 41223 arrives at Bradwell station on the Newport Pagnell branch with a 'push-pull' service on 12th May 1962. The branch was constructed in 1866 from the WCML at Wolverton to Newport Pagnell, with two stations at Bradwell and Great Linford. The line seen curving away on the right had been in use for a private siding from around the time of the inauguration of services and was used for a variety of businesses, latterly for a scrap merchant; the white sign forbids locomotives from going any further due to the curvature of the line being the potential cause of a derailment.

Opposite above **BRAUNSTON & WILLOUGHBY**

Standard Class 9F no. 92076 at Braunston & Willoughby with an Up coal train on 24th May 1958.

Opposite below **BROMSGROVE STATION**

Fowler 'Patriot' Class 4-6-0 no. 45504 *Royal Signals* passes through Bromsgrove station with the 14.15 Bristol Temple Meads to York on 18th August 1960.

Above **BROUGHTON ASTLEY STATION**

At the southern end of the Midland Counties Railway line from Long Eaton to Rugby was Broughton Astley station. From opening on 30th June 1840 the station was predominantly known as Broughton before Astley was used during the 1850s and 1860s. After disappearing again during the 1870s, Broughton Astley was the full title until closure on 1st January 1962. Just eight months before this event (24th April 1961) Fowler 4P Class 2-6-4T no. 42352 has been pictured with a Rugby to Leicester local service.

Opposite above **BROMSGROVE STATION**

Bromsgrove station was at the bottom of Lickey incline, therefore was a place where trains acquired bankers to help them up to the top. Johnson Class M (LMSR 3F) 0-6-0 no. 43762 has two pushing from the rear of this long Up freight on 18th August 1960. The locomotive was constructed by Neilson, Reid & Co. in August 1902 as one of the final class members. After spending much of the early 1950s at Saltley shed, the engine's final allocation from April 1956 was Bromsgrove and withdrawal occurred in March 1961.

Opposite below **BROOKSBY STATION**

The Syston & Peterborough Railway was promoted in the 1840s to connect the Midland Counties Railway (later part of the MR) at Syston (north of Leicester) with Peterborough via Melton Mowbray and Stamford. Most of the line was ready in 1846 and one of the stations was Brooksby, which was located a short distance north east of Syston. The services on the line were scaled back in the 1950s and Brooksby was a casualty in July 1961, but the line remains open today for cross-country traffic — the station also remains intact as a private residence. On 4th June 1962 Stanier 8F no. 48651 travels through with an iron-ore train.

Above **BURNLEY ROSE GROVE SHED**
No. 45397 leads a line-up of Stanier Class 5s at Burnley Rose Grove shed on 29th July 1966.

Opposite above **BURNLEY CENTRAL STATION**
The late 1840s saw a flurry of projects undertaken by the East Lancashire Railway that ultimately connected Preston with Colne via Blackburn, Accrington and Burnley. The latter town's station was open for traffic from 1st December 1848 following the completion of the final section from there to Colne. Initially known as Burnley, the station's name later received the appendage 'Bank Top' in the early 1870s, then 'Central' in 1944 which currently remains in use. This view was captured from Colne Road on 20th September 1962.

Opposite below **BURSCOUGH JUNCTION STATION**
Burscough Junction station was opened on 2nd April 1849 on the line from Liverpool to Preston via Ormskirk and pre-dated Burscough Bridge station built for the Manchester-Southport services in 1855. At this date the name changed from Burscough to Burscough Junction as connections were possible with the latter line, although this is no longer the case. Stanier Class 5 no. 44733 has an express from Windermere bound for Liverpool on 26th August 1964.

Above **CARLISLE**

The forerunner of the 'Caledonian' express was the 'Coronation Scot' streamline train and for which new locomotives were designed. Stanier's 'Coronation' Class Pacifics were an improvement on the earlier 'Princess Royals' and five were built initially to be used exclusively with the new train. Eventually orders were placed for engines to run on normal expresses and up to 1948 a total of 38 were constructed. No. 46250 *City of Lichfield* was erected late in the war and was in traffic until October 1964. The engine is seen here from London Road Bridge at Carlisle heading south on 12th August 1960.

Opposite above **CARLISLE CITADEL STATION**

At the north end of Carlisle Citadel station Ivatt Class 4MT 2-6-0 no. 43049 loiters in the middle road, whilst Fowler 3F Class 0-6-0T no. 47326 is at work on pilot duties on 7th May 1965. Both locomotives had some time left in service, with the older 3F (built in July 1926 by the North British Locomotive Co.) going first in December 1966, followed by no. 43049 (constructed at Horwich Works in November 1949) during August 1967.

Opposite below **CARLISLE CITADEL STATION**

In the early 1930s the Pacific (4-6-2) type wheel arrangement was finally adopted by the LMSR for express services. Two were produced initially in 1933 and a further ten entered traffic in 1935. Seen here approaching Carlisle Citadel station from the north with the 10.15 Glasgow to Euston (with coaches for Plymouth, which detached at Crewe) on 12th August 1960, no. 46201 *Princess Elizabeth* was the second class member to be completed at Crewe Works in November 1933 and remained in service until October 1962. Almost a year later the engine was bought from BR and preserved; no. 46201 has recently undergone a major overhaul.

Above **CHESTER GENERAL STATION**

Stanier Class 5 no. 44834 draws up to the Down main platform, which is busy with summer holidaymakers, at Chester General station with the 09.06 Birmingham New Street to Holyhead on 22nd July 1961.

Opposite above **CHESTER GENERAL STATION**

At the east end of Chester General station on 4th August 1962 three services are lined up and waiting to depart once Chester No. 2 signal box (seen in the distance) gives them the road. Nearest the camera is BR Standard Class 4 2-6-0 no. 76089 which has the 12.30 from Abergele to Manchester Victoria, on the right a DMU has a service to North Wales and on the far side is Stanier Class 5 4-6-0, which is also at the head of an express for North Wales.

Opposite below **CHESTER GENERAL STATION**

Three locomotives coupled together run through Chester General station on the Down main line on 16th September 1965. Leading is BR Standard Class 9F no. 92024, which was formerly fitted with a Franco-Crosti boiler, followed by a Stanier Class 5 and another 9F.

Below CHESTER GENERAL STATION

When Stanier arrived on the LMSR in the early 1930s he brought from Swindon Works a more 'modern' outlook to locomotive design. One of the designs he soon introduced was the 8F 2-8-0 for the heavy duties across the system and a total of 852 would be erected from 1935 to 1946. No. 48344 was one of 75 built at Horwich Works between 1943 and 1945, being completed in March 1944. In the early 1950s the locomotive spent time at Shrewsbury shed and at the end of the decade was working from Chester West shed. When photographed on the through line at Chester General station on 16th September 1965, no. 48344 had been at Trafford Park for several years but would be withdrawn from Heaton Mersey shed after less than a month there in April 1968.

Above **CHESTER GENERAL STATION**

Two stations were replaced by the opening of Chester Joint (General from the 1870s) on 1st August 1848. The first was the Birkenhead, Lancashire & Cheshire Junction Railway's terminus on 23rd September 1840 which was located a short distance away to the west of the later station. Following on only a few days later was the Chester & Crewe Railway facility and this was sited to the east. With the Chester & Holyhead Railway being envisaged in the mid-1840s, a new station was planned for use of all three companies. This was designed by Francis Thompson in the Italianate style which was prevalent in railway architecture at the time. Arriving at the west end of the station on 29th August 1964 is BR Standard Class 5 no. 73140, which is fitted with Caprotti valve gear, and the train is the 12.20 from Holyhead to Manchester Exchange.

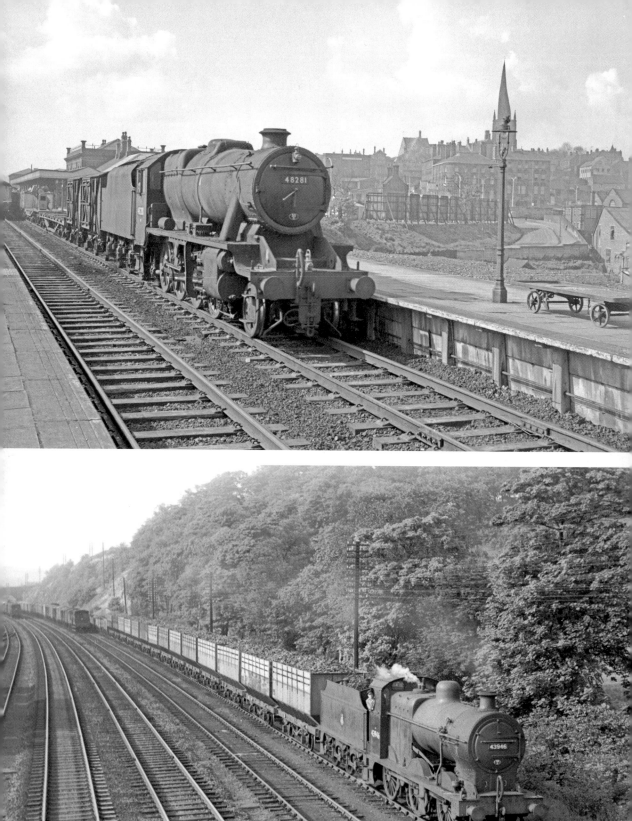

Above CHINLEY SOUTH JUNCTION

The Goyt Valley and High Peak provide the scenic backdrop for Stanier 'Jubilee' Class no. 45598 *Basutoland*, which passes Chinley South Junction with the 16.25 Manchester Central to St Pancras express on 19th June 1957. The line curving away to the right is the Hope Valley line to Sheffield and this section remains open to provide the link to Manchester; the line the locomotive is taking to the south, which connected with the Midland main line at Ambergate Junction, was closed past Blackwell in 1967.

Opposite above CHESTERFIELD MIDLAND STATION

The North Midland Railway skirted past Chesterfield's eastern side on the way from Derby to Leeds and a station was opened for the town on 11th May 1840. Thirty years later a new station was completed a short distance away, but this has since been rebuilt twice, although remaining on the same site. The first occurred a short time after this image of Stanier 8F no. 48281 (travelling north with a mixed freight) was captured on 24th April 1961, looking south west to the famous St Mary and All Saints Church with the 'crooked spire'. In 1963 the station was replaced by one in BR's style of the period and during the 1990s this too was changed for a new design. For a brief ten years from 1951 Chesterfield station had 'Midland' added to the title to help passengers distinguish between the town's three stations.

Opposite below CHESTERFIELD

With the main line dividing a short distance north of Chesterfield, the section before the junction was always busy with trains off the Sheffield deviation and those from the original route. Here, Fowler 3F 0-6-0 no. 43946 takes the Up slow goods line south towards Chesterfield station on 13th June 1957 and is in charge of a train of ex-LMSR 20-ton coke hopper wagons. With the large number of collieries in the area there was a perpetual flow of this traffic on the main line.

Above **CHINLEY STATION**

For much of the history of the steam locomotive, attempts had been made to harness some of the energy present in exhaust steam, which was usually lost to the atmosphere, through various pieces of apparatus. Shortly after Grouping trials were made by the LMSR of Davies & Metcalfe exhaust steam injectors which siphoned off exhaust from the blastpipe and returned the steam to the boiler thereby reducing fuel consumption. This was unsuccessful but following modifications to the equipment orders were given to replace the ordinary injectors with the exhaust injectors. When built at Derby Works in May 1925 Fowler 4F Class no. 4054 (later no. 44054 from 1950) was fitted with two Gresham & Craven live-steam injectors, but was later fitted with the Davies & Metcalfe pattern. The pipe can be seen exiting the smokebox and going under the running plate to an oil separator — visible between the intermediate and rear coupled wheels — before entering the boiler from the injector. No. 44054 advances westward with a mineral train through Chinley station on 19th June 1957.

Below CHINLEY SOUTH JUNCTION

The Peak District has notable sandstone deposits which have been mined for many years. Tunstead Quarry was established just south of Peak Dale in the late 1920s and has been in continuous production ever since. Stanier 8F no. 48521 appears to be heading there with a train of empty stone hopper wagons on 19th June 1957. The engine is seen at Chinley South Junction looking north east, with the two viaducts carrying the line from Sheffield (right) and Manchester (left) over the Black Brook also featuring. Sandstone and cement trains continue to run to the quarry using this part of the old Midland route.

Above **CREWE WORKS**

LNWR 'Special Tank' 0-6-0ST no. 3323 spent many years in the service of Crewe Works and is pictured there on 2nd May 1948. Only five of the 260 built survived at this time and this example would not be scrapped until 1954.

Below **CREWE NORTH SHED**

Stanier 'Princess Royal' Pacific no. 6210 *Lady Patricia* at Crewe North shed, 2nd May 1948. Built in September 1935, the locomotive spent 13 years working from the shed from 1943 to 1956.

Above **CREWE WORKS**

The dramatic damage was sustained by no. 6251 *City of Nottingham* at Winsford (between Crewe and Northwich). A soldier pulled the communication cord to get off the 17.40 Glasgow-Euston passenger train and take a short cut home. No. 6251 on the following 'West Coast Postal' collided with the rear of the passenger train at 40 mph, killing 24, after a signalman let the train into the section in error. Repair is awaited at Crewe Works on 2nd May 1948.

Below **CREWE WORKS**

Another old LNWR engine — 0-4-2ST no. 7862 — is in use for shunting at Crewe Works, 2nd May 1948.

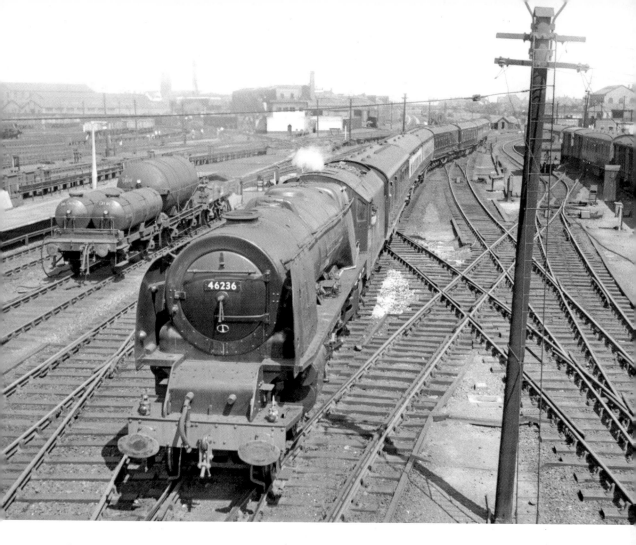

Above **CREWE STATION**

No. 46236 *City of Bradford* is on the 10.15 Manchester London Road to Bournemouth West at Crewe on 19th June 1957. The mobile gas cylinders on the left stand ready to replenish the reservoirs of kitchen-car stock.

Opposite above **CREWE STATION**

At the north end of Crewe station two important lines can be seen joining the WCML, which runs through the centre. On the right is the route to Manchester (opened by the Manchester & Birmingham Railway in 1840) and on the left is the line from Chester. Coming off the latter on 19th July 1958 is the 13.20 Llandudno to Derby express which has Stanier 'Jubilee' Class no. 45700 *Amethyst* piloting Class 5 no. 45026. Both locomotives were allocated to sheds off the route of the train as no. 45700 was based at Bank Hall, Liverpool, and no. 45026 was at Wigan Springs Branch depot. There are plenty of 'platform enders' to record the train's arrival.

Opposite below **CREWE STATION**

A footbridge over the north end of Crewe station again provides the vantage point for a view of two locomotives working together. This image dates from 19th June 1957 and sees Stanier 'Jubilee' no. 45722 *Defence* piloting classmate no. 45592 *Indore* on the 07.55 Euston to Liverpool Lime Street which trails behind along platform one. Only the first mentioned was a product of Crewe Works, which was located to the west of the station alongside the Chester line, *Indore* being completed by the NBLC 20 months earlier than *Defence* in December 1934. In front of the locomotives is Crewe North signal box which was installed in 1940, being built from reinforced concrete to limit any potential damage caused by air raids, and had a frame operated by small levers supplied by Westinghouse. This was in use until the mid-1980s and has subsequently become an exhibit at Crewe Heritage Centre.

Above **CREWE STATION**

Moving to the south end of Crewe station on 19th July 1958, BR Standard Class 3MT 2-6-2T no. 82009 has just brought in a local service from Wellington, while Stanier Class 5 no. 45394 stands behind with the 10.50 Workington to Euston. No. 82009 was allocated to Wellington shed at this time and had three years there from 1956, having been sent to Tyseley when new from Swindon in June 1952 and followed by spells at Barry and Newton Abbot. The early 1960s would be spent in the Bristol and South Wales areas; the engine was condemned from Patricroft shed in November 1966.

Opposite above **CREWE STATION**

After the successful introduction of Fowler's 'Royal Scot' Class on the LMSR's heavy main-line expresses, the company's other inter-city services were deemed to be in need of new motive power of similar design but with a wider route availability. Two prototypes for the new class, which was later designated the 'Patriot' Class, were produced at Derby in 1930 and followed by another 50 between 1932 and 1934. No. 45527 *Southport* was erected at Crewe Works in March 1933, taking the original number (5527) from a withdrawn 'Claughton', but the name was new and was bestowed on the engine in 1937 to publicise the places served by the LMSR. The locomotive was later rebuilt with a new Stanier-type boiler (amongst other modifications) in September 1948. Passing by Stanier Class 5 no. 45282, *Southport* is travelling southward through Crewe station with an unidentified special on 13th June 1959.

Opposite below **CREWE STATION**

This 'Jubilee' Class locomotive, no. 45595 *Southern Rhodesia*, is seen back in steam following a general repair at Crewe Works, being pictured on the north-west side of the station on 20th June 1957. Based at Longsight shed at this time, and for much of the early 1950s, the engine would be allocated to Crewe North shed — the 'Middle shed' and the site were located behind the locomotive — for five years from June 1959 to September 1964. Withdrawal from Llandudno Junction occurred four months later in January 1965; no. 45595 had accumulated over 1 million miles in service.

Above **DERBY WORKS**

A busy scene in Derby Works Erecting Shop on Wednesday, 13th April 1960. On the right closest to the camera is 4F no. 44289 and on the left — looking relatively complete — is Fowler 4P 2-6-4T no. 42311.

Opposite above **DERBY SHED**

Sunday, 2nd April 1950, is a rest day for these three 0-6-0 locomotives which are seen at Derby shed. Johnson 3F no. 43572 (still with LMS on the tender) is on the far right, Fowler 4F no. 44412, which was based at Nottingham at the time, is in the middle and on the left is another 4F, no. 43879 of Saltley. The 4Fs mentioned, were both constructed at Derby Works which is on the right.

Opposite Middle **DERBY WORKS**

Several locomotives are lined up on the Foundry Road at Derby Works on 2nd April 1950 for repair, although two would not return to traffic. Leading the line is 2F 0-6-0 no. 22853, which was condemned, followed by 2F 0-6-0 no. 22913, 1P 0-4-4T no. 58041 (withdrawn), 3P 2-6-2T no. 40037, 4P Compound 4-4-0 no. 41044, 3F 0-6-0 no. 43482 and 4F 0-6-0 no. 44584.

Opposite below **DERBY SHED**

Four Stanier locomotives are accommodated outside Derby shed and are seen here grouped around the turntable on 2nd April 1950. They are (left to right): 'Jubilee' no. 45664 *Nelson*; Class Fives, no. 44853, no. 44819 and no. 44856.

Above **DERBY STATION**

All lines at Derby station are occupied in this hectic scene captured towards the end of steam, 4th May 1965. A train is present on the platform line, BR Type 2 diesel D7585 stands on the second track from right, Class 5 no. 44766 the third, a train with a flat wagon the fourth and partially in the view is BR Standard Class 2 no. 78064.

Opposite above **DERBY STATION**

BR introduced several Standard Classes after Nationalisation to meet motive power shortages that were similar on most of the Regions. Many of these new designs were heavily influenced by those produced by the LMSR, one being H.G. Ivatt's Class 2 2-6-0 which was introduced in 1946. A total of 65 Standard Class 2s were erected — all at Darlington Works — and spread across the country, although none was initially allocated to the Eastern or Southern Regions. No. 78057 was completed in September 1956 and allocated to Chester, spending the following eight years in and around the area before moving south to Derby in May 1964. The locomotive has been pictured at the station on 24th June 1964 when employed as the station pilot. From March 1965 to withdrawal in May 1966 no. 78057 was based at Lostock Hall shed (south of Preston).

Opposite below **DERBY WORKS**

Three locomotives are in various stages of their demise at Derby Works on 13th April 1960. The most advanced is no. 44406, constructed by the NBLC in January 1927 and condemned in March 1960 at Saltley shed. Classmate no. 44515 has similarly lost the boiler clothing plates but the asbestos lagging remains in place. This locomotive was erected at Crewe Works in June 1928 and was also withdrawn from Saltley. Fowler Class 3P 2-6-2T no. 40070 — built at Derby in November 1932 —appears to be relatively intact and was recently taken out of service from Willesden.

Above **DUFFIELD**

North of Duffield, Hughes 'Crab' Class 2-6-0 no. 42874 heads south with a freight train in mid-June 1957. In the distance is the two-track Milford Tunnel, although the beginnings of the four-track section are seen here; on the Down line is another freight train disappearing into the portal.

Below **ECCLES JUNCTION**

Fowler 3F Class 0-6-0T no. 47365 shunts empty coal wagons at Eccles Junction, Patricroft station on 18th April 1962. For much of the BR period the locomotive was allocated to Patricroft shed.

Above **FARINGTON EAST JUNCTION**

'Austerity' Class 2-8-0 no. 90163 leads a train of flat wagons past Farington East Junction on 10th September 1962. This was the location for a spur to the Blackburn-Liverpool line from the WCML. In the distance on the right is the mechanical coaler for Lostock Hall depot.

Below **FARINGTON STATION**

Stanier Class 5 no. 44965 approaches Farington station on the Down fast line with the 16.55 Manchester Victoria to Blackpool North on 20th June 1957.

Above FRODSHAM STATION

Frodsham station was opened on 18th December 1850 by the Birkenhead, Lancashire & Cheshire Railway on the line between Chester and the LNWR line south of Warrington. The 10.31 express from Manchester to Bangor is seen at the station behind Stanier Class 5 no. 45044 on 22nd August 1964.

Opposite above GLAZEBROOK STATION

The Cheshire Lines Committee was founded in the early 1860s by the Great Northern Railway and Manchester, Sheffield & Lincolnshire Railway (later Great Central Railway) to break the stranglehold the LNWR had on lines in the Manchester/Liverpool/Chester area. The CLC operated absorbed lines initially before turning to construction in the early 1870s with a new line from Manchester to Liverpool. Glazebrook station was built with the line and opened on 1st September 1873. With the 13.30 express from Manchester Central to Liverpool Central just west of the station is Stanier 4MT 2-6-4T no. 42448 on 21st June 1957.

Below **HARTFORD**

Stanier 8F no. 48255 takes the spur off the CLC's Manchester/Northwich/Chester line to join the WCML just north of Hartford with a soda-ash train from ICI Northwich on 12th April 1966.

Above **HARTFORD STATION**

As the introduction of Fowler's 'Patriot' Class 4-6-0s was imminent when Stanier took over he allowed those on order to be completed comparatively unaltered. When further orders were required he chose to put his own ideas into a design — the 'Jubilee' Class 4-6-0. A total of 191 were completed in just three years between 1934 and 1936; no. 45613 *Kenya* emerged from Crewe Works in August 1934. There were often variations between batches and ten successive locomotives — including no. 45613 — at this time were fitted with high-sided tenders based on a Fowler design with a coal capacity of 7 tons and room for 3,500 gallons of water. A noticeable feature of these, and with other Fowler-type tenders fitted to the class, was the discrepancy in width between them and the engine. No. 45613 is seen just north of Hartford station with a Down semi-fitted freight on 21st June 1957.

Below **HARTFORD STATION**

As part of BR's Modernisation Plan of 1955 part of the WCML between Crewe and Weaver Junction was electrified with a 25 kV AC system, along with the section from there to Liverpool and from Crewe to Manchester. The latter was completed first in 1960 and followed by Crewe-Liverpool which began operating at the start of 1962. Here at Hartford on 22nd May 1961 construction work on new station buildings and the overhead gantries and wires progresses for this event. Stopping at Hartford with a local service is 'Patriot' Class 4-6-0 no. 45543 *Home Guard*, which was constructed at Crewe Works in March 1934 and condemned for scrap in November 1962.

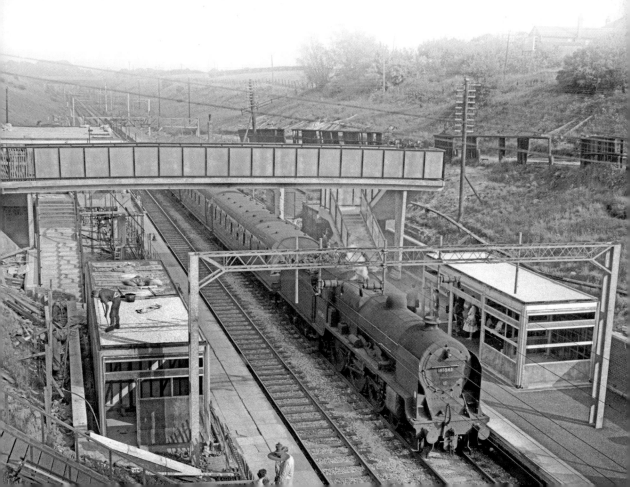

Above HARTFORD, HODGE LANE

View north west from Hodge Lane, Hartford, as WD 'Austerity' no. 90135 comes off the WCML to join the CLC route between Chester and Manchester with a train of empties on 27th December 1961. The locomotive was allocated to Mirfield shed at this time and was there between July 1961 and March 1964.

Opposite above HASSOP STATION

Stanier's 8F 2-8-0 design was adopted by the War Department as a standard freight design in 1939 and the works of the 'Big Four' were employed building them. Interestingly, the London & North Eastern Railway decided to build 100 to ease their own motive power shortages but in the event 68 were only completed. No. 48770 was built at Doncaster in May 1946 as LNER no. 3165 and worked for the company until September 1947 when transferred to the LMSR. The engine is seen on 23rd June 1961 working through Hassop station (on the MR's Ambergate to Manchester line) with a train of empty coaching stock. Closed to passengers in August 1942, Hassop remained open to freight until October 1964 but has survived subsequently as a cafe.

Opposite below HASSOP STATION

On the same day as the picture of no. 48770 the camera has been turned north-west from the vantage point of the B6001 road bridge over the line. Captured with an Up empties is 4F Class no. 44038 which was constructed at Derby Works in January 1925 and in service until April 1964.

Above KILLAMARSH, STATION ROAD

View north from Station Road bridge, Killamarsh, as 8F no. 48439 steams past with an Up coal train on 14th September 1957. The locomotive was built at Swindon Works for the War Department in May 1944 and was then loaned to the Great Western Railway until early 1947. From Nationalisation to withdrawal in November 1967 the engine was allocated to Royston shed.

Opposite above KILLAMARSH STATION

From 1954 the ex-North Midland Railway line between Chesterfield and Treeton (east of Sheffield) was closed to passenger traffic and dedicated to freight traffic — a role that continues today — to reduce the strain on the line through Sheffield. Nevertheless, excursion and holiday traffic was sometimes routed on the 'old road' if the deviation through Sheffield was unnecessary. This was the case for the 09.25 from Filey Holiday Camp which is travelling to King's Norton (south of Birmingham) through Killamarsh station on 13th July 1963. In charge of the express is 'Jubilee' Class no. 45676 *Codrington* which was built at Crewe in December 1935 and withdrawn in September 1964.

Opposite below HELLIFIELD STATION

From the late 1880s and through the 1890s the MR experienced a near continuous growth in goods traffic, resulting in many orders for Johnson's 'Standard Goods' 0-6-0. No. 43585 was built at the tail-end of the run by Kitson & Co. in October 1899 as MR no. 2406 and possessing a boiler with a round-top firebox, but this latter has subsequently been replaced by the Belpaire type. The locomotive is seen shunting empty carriages at Hellifield station on 8th June 1959; withdrawal from service would occur in September 1962.

Above **KIRKHAM & WESHAM STATION**

BR Standard Pacific no. 70043 *Lord Kitchener* charges westward to Blackpool through Kirkham & Wesham station with an 'Illuminations' special on 8th September 1962.

Opposite above **KIRKHAM & WESHAM STATION**

At Nationalisation there were thousands of engines in need of replacement. Branch line services were perhaps the most affected and as a result BR took inspiration for a suitable design from the recently introduced LMSR Ivatt 2-6-2T. BR's Standard Class 2 2-6-2T appeared in 1953 when 20 were erected at Crewe Works, followed by another 10 in 1957 from Darlington. No. 84018 was turned out from Crewe in October 1953 and initially allocated to Bury, but several months later was moved to Fleetwood, where the engine remained until withdrawn in April 1965. The locomotive has been photographed on 8th September 1962 with a local train from Fleetwood stopping at Kirkham & Wesham station.

Opposite below **KIRKBY-IN-ASHFIELD STATION**

Another MR expansion project in the mid-1840s was the connection of villages north of Nottingham and the town of Kirkby-in-Ashfield. This was completed in October 1848, with an extension to Mansfield following on soon in 1849. For 25 years this was the end of the line, but a new section to Worksop on the GCR Manchester-Lincoln route was constructed in the early 1870s and open for traffic in 1875. The same period coincided with great industrial growth in the area — namely several coal mines being established along the line — and the MR was in a prime position to benefit. The GNR's line from Nottingham to Shirebrook and later the GCR's London Extension also sought to claim the riches from the coal traffic. Kirkby-in-Ashfield was a point of convergence for all three lines, although only the GCR and MR had stations there. Heading north through the latter company's facility is 4F no. 44531 on 13th July 1963. The station would only remain open until October of the following year when the Nottingham to Worksop line would become freight-only. Passenger services have since returned to the route, which has become an amalgamation of the GNR and MR lines and a new Kirkby-in-Ashfield station has been opened on the GNR route to the west.

Below KIRKHAM & WESHAM STATION

Kirkham & Wesham station was opened as Kirkham by the Preston & Wyre Railway & Dock Co. on 16th July 1840. The station was one of only two intermediate stops between the WCML at Preston and the port at Fleetwood, but additions were later made. There were also branches off the original route, two being immediately east of Kirkham & Wesham. The first was to Lytham St Annes in 1861 (subsequently extending further up the coast to Blackpool) and at the turn of the century the Marton Line was laid to give direct access to Blackpool, which had been reached circuitously beforehand. Stanier 'Jubilee' Class no. 45694 *Bellerophon* is signalled to take the Marton Line with an 'Illuminations' special from Bradford on 8th September 1962. The locomotive had only recently transferred from Leeds Holbeck shed having spent the previous 20 years there. Another five years in traffic were ahead for the engine, three being at Bradford Low Moor and the final two at Wakefield.

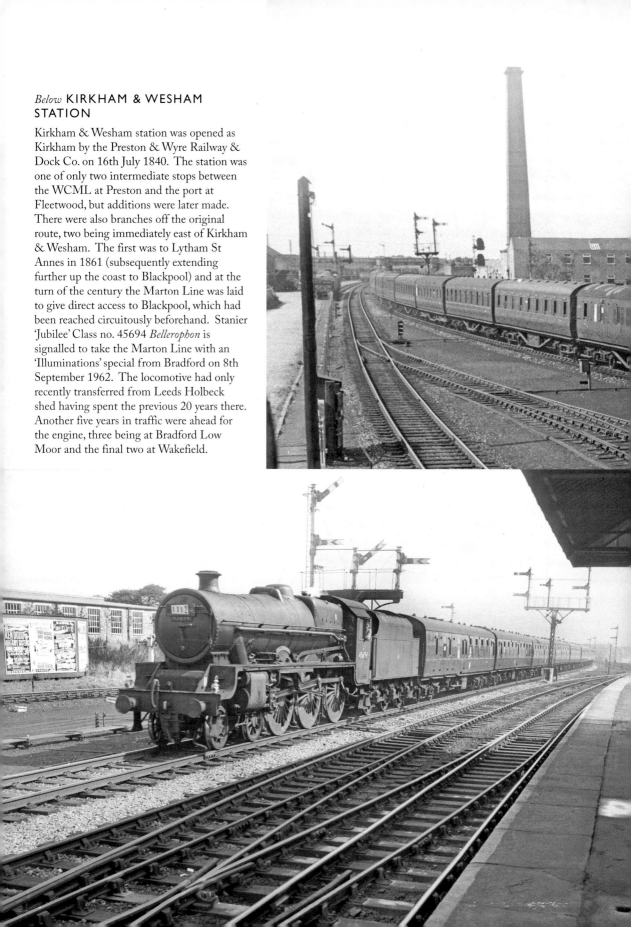

Above **KIRKHAM & WESHAM STATION**

The 12.50 Blackpool Central to Manchester Victoria station local service arrives at Kirkham & Wesham behind Stanier Class 5 no. 44930. The picture has been taken — on 8th September 1962 — from Station Road bridge looking west towards Kirkham Junction where the Lytham line diverged and a short distance further on the Marton and Fleetwood lines split off. The Marton route was closed in 1965 and the trackbed has been reused for a roadway. The Phoenix Mill is behind the first two carriages and has subsequently been demolished to make way for a biscuit factory.

Above LEEDS CITY STATION

The Railway Correspondence & Travel Society's 'The Borders' railtour was organised for 9th July 1961 to run from Leeds City station to Carlisle, then via the Waverley route to St Boswells. From there the Kelso branch was taken to meet the East Coast Main line at Tweedmouth. The jaunt then proceeded to Newcastle and back to Leeds City. On the first leg from Leeds was Stanier 'Coronation' Class Pacific no. 46247 *City of Liverpool* — the only LMR representative — which then handed over to a Thompson B1 Class 4-6-0 at Carlisle. In the Borders the motive power was the preserved D34 Class 4-4-0 no. 256 *Glen Douglas* with a J37, but on the ECML a switch was made to a Peppercorn A1 and later a Gresley A3.

Opposite above LANGLEY MILL & EASTWOOD STATION

An Up train of empty coal wagons trundles along the Erewash Valley line towards Langley Mill & Eastwood station on 13th April 1960. No. 44321 was based locally at Westhouses shed (north of Alfreton) and had been there from the mid-1940s, remaining until condemned during April 1964. The station was closed a short time later in 1967 but reopened on the same site as Langley Mill in 1986.

Opposite below LEA GREEN STATION

The main line between Manchester Exchange and Liverpool Lime Street was relatively level apart from a five-mile stretch between St Helens Junction and Huyton Quarry where there was a distinct hump. Stanier Class 5 no. 45196 appears to be struggling on the eastern rise of 1 in 91 for 1½ miles to Lea Green station and has the help of an 0-6-0T banker at the rear of the freight train to reach the top on 16th April 1962.

Above LEICESTER SHED

With the opening of the line in 1840, the MCR also provided a roundhouse locomotive shed on the east side of the main line just north of the station. A short time later a new roundhouse was added to the original on the eastern side and by the turn of the century a three-road straight shed had been built to further improve the accommodation. All three lasted until 1945 when the site was extensively rebuilt by the LMSR and a new large roundhouse was erected along with the mechanical coalers, one of which is seen here servicing a Class 5 on 29th September 1957. The shed was closed to steam in 1965 and a diesel servicing facility was built; the site remains in railway use at present.

Opposite above LEICESTER LONDON ROAD STATION

Leicester London Road station was the first to serve the city when opened by the Midland Counties Railway on 5th May 1840. The GNR and GCR subsequently established their own stations, forcing the MR to distinguish their facility by the addition of 'London Road' to the title and this was in use between 1892 and 1970. On the eastern side of the station looking north, two locomotives are seen on 23rd June 1961. Adjacent to the water column is Fairburn Class 4MT 2-6-4T no. 42103 and at the platform is Fowler 4F no. 44575 with the 20.45 local service to Northampton via Market Harborough.

Opposite below LEICESTER SHED

View from Hutchinson Street to Leicester locomotive yard, shed (partially obscured on the right), goods depot and main line to the north on 29th September 1957. In the foreground are two 0-6-0s, 3F no. 43710 (left) and 4F no. 44522; behind is 8F 2-8-0 no. 48553. Standing close to the two mechanical coalers is 'Crab' Class 2-6-0 no. 42733 and Stanier Class 5 no. 45137, while on the opposite side are representatives of BR's Standard designs, an Ivatt Class 2 2-6-0 and older 0-6-0s. In the mid-1950s the depot had over 70 locomotives allocated to cover passenger and freight duties in the area.

Above **LEIGHTON BUZZARD STATION**

Webb Class 2 0-6-2T no. 6917 is at the head of a Dunstable branch train at Leighton Buzzard on 2nd October 1948. The locomotive was built at Crewe Works in May 1901 and withdrawn during 1949.

Below **LEIGHTON BUZZARD SHED**

Ex-LNWR 'Super D' Class 0-8-0 no. 48953 is partially accommodated in the engine shed at Leighton Buzzard on 10th April 1960. Despite half of the roof being recently replaced, the shed would soon close.

Above **LEYLAND STATION**

The 16.00 Blackpool Central to Manchester Exchange (consisting of just four carriages) is headed by two Stanier Class 5s, no. 45318 and no. 45195. The train has been pictured at Leyland station on 17th August 1963.

Below **LEYLAND STATION**

Also passing through Leyland station on the same day as above was rebuilt 'Patriot' Class no. 45512 *Bunsen*, which has an Up parcels. The locomotive had 18 months left in service.

Above LICHFIELD TRENT VALLEY (LOW LEVEL) STATION

Initially 58 Stanier 'Jubilee' Class 4-6-0s were ordered from Crewe and Derby for completion during 1934. The realisation was soon made that these would not be ready so an order for another 50 was placed with the North British Locomotive Co. for delivery in April 1934. This target was passed by two months before the first engine arrived and the delivery of the remainder crawled into 1935. No. 45603 *Solomon Islands* was one of the final locomotives in the order to be erected by the NBLC's Queens Park Works in late January 1935, although (for undisclosed reasons) the LMSR did not deem the engine ready for service until mid-May 1935. This made the engine the last of the batch to be officially in traffic by a month. No. 45603 is seen hard at work here approaching Lichfield Trent Valley (Low Level) with a Down freight on 4th June 1962.

Opposite LICHFIELD TRENT VALLEY (LOW LEVEL) STATION

Arriving at Lichfield Trent Valley (Low Level) station on 4th June 1962 — under the watchful eye of the station inspector (in the foreground with hat) — is an express from Manchester London Road to Euston. The station was the crossing point for the Stafford to Rugby line, which was opened first in 1847, and the Dudley to Burton-on-Trent route, built in 1849. Originally two separate stations were used, but after the initiating companies became part of the LNWR new High Level and Low Level stations were opened in 1871. The latter is seen here looking north west and the former was located behind the camera. In the shot is rebuilt 'Royal Scot' no. 46156 *The South Wales Borderer* which was erected at Derby in October 1930, named a year later, rebuilt in mid-1954 and withdrawn in October 1964. The engine was working from Holyhead when pictured and would be based at Willesden, then Annesley before condemned.

Above **LICKEY INCLINE**

At the top of Lickey freight trains were obliged to stop and have all the hand brakes on the wagons pinned down to prevent a runaway occurring. Johnson 3F Class 0-6-0 no. 43210 is leading these vans and wagons down on 26th April 1957. The locomotive was erected by Neilson & Co. in February 1890 as no. 1883 and would remain in traffic until August 1959.

Opposite above **LICKEY INCLINE**

The Lickey Incline was one of the most challenging in the country, being 1 in 37 for two miles from Bromsgrove to Blackwell on the Birmingham to Bristol line. BR 9F 2-10-0 no. 92136 is making progress with a fully-laden oil train from Fawley Refinery, near Southampton, to Bromford Bridge, Birmingham, on 16th August 1963 with the aid of four 94XX Class 0-6-0T locomotives at the rear. No. 92136 was constructed at Crewe Works in July 1957 and was allocated to Saltley shed until condemned in October 1966.

Opposite below **LICKEY INCLINE**

With a constant stream of passenger and freight traffic moving between Birmingham and Bristol there was always a need for banking engines. At the top of the Lickey Incline (on 14th April 1949) are five which have worked to the top and have accumulated in order to return to Bromsgrove together. All are Fowler 3F Class 0-6-0Ts and from the front they are: no. 47425, no. 47303, no. 47313, no. 47301 and no. 47305. All except no. 47313 spent much of the 1950s at work on the section before being transferred away when the Western Region took over Bromsgrove shed in 1958 and replaced by 94XX Class locomotives.

Above LICKEY INCLINE

A large number of Stanier Class 5s had been introduced before the war to replace older and obsolete classes, but more were still necessary. The start of the conflict delayed further orders being placed until June 1943 when 55 were authorised, followed by another 105 in November. These were requested from Derby, Crewe and Horwich Works, with the latter being responsible for no. 44966, pictured, although the original tender was produced at Derby. The locomotive was in fact the last of the 1943 orders to be completed in August 1946 and went new to Saltley shed. No. 44966 was still based there when seen on Lickey Incline with an Up relief express from Bristol on 19th April 1949 and, after a five-month spell allocated to Bristol from December 1956, would maintain an association with Saltley until 1964 when moved to Holyhead. Withdrawal from Shrewsbury occurred in September 1966.

Opposite LICKEY INCLINE

The success of mixed traffic 2-6-0s on several railways in Britain inspired George Hughes, new CME of the LMSR after Grouping (previously heading the locomotive department of the Lancashire & Yorkshire Railway) to design his own locomotive for use on the company's services. The result was a large, powerful locomotive with several L&YR features. A total of 100 were initially ordered and the first appeared in 1926 to be followed by orders for a further 145 and these were erected up to 1932. No. 42846 was one of 20 authorised in mid-1930 and constructed at Horwich between then and the end of the year; as no. 13146 this engine was completed in late October and first allocated to Derby. Renumbered 2846 in September 1935, the locomotive moved to Burton-on-Trent in August 1937 and remained there until August 1954. Then, no. 42846 took a berth at Saltley shed until November 1960 when a transfer to Gorton occurred. This event was just a short time away when the locomotive was pictured on Lickey Incline with a train of mineral empties on 18th August 1960.

Above **LIVERPOOL BANK HALL SHED**

No. 45225 — the first Class 5 built at Armstrong Whitworth in July 1936 — is seen fresh from a general repair and back working from Liverpool Bank Hall shed on 20th June 1948.

Below **LINSLADE**

Webb 0-8-0 no. 49352 heads a freight towards Linslade tunnel (west of Leighton Buzzard) on the WCML on 2nd October 1948. The engine was originally part of the B Class but was rebuilt to G2A specifications.

Above **LIVERPOOL BANK HALL SHED**

Two former L&YR locomotives are seen outside the company's smaller shed at Bank Hall, Liverpool, on 20th June 1948. On the right is Aspinall 24 Class 0-6-0T no. 11535 and to the left is Class 30 0-8-0 no. 12782.

Below **LIVERPOOL BANK HALL SHED**

Also at Bank Hall shed, on the same day as the picture above, is L&YR Aspinall 21 Class 0-4-0ST no. 11246, which would have been employed in one of the many goods yards around Liverpool. A 4-4-0 receives attention in the background.

LIVERPOOL EDGE HILL SIDINGS

View north east to Edge Hill sidings, Liverpool, from Picton Road bridge as the 09.00 from Hull via Leeds and Manchester approaches behind 'Jubilee' Class no. 45695 *Minotaur* on 12th June 1959. The extensive Edge Hill sidings handled the vast majority of the traffic to and from Waterloo and Park Lane goods stations, as well as Liverpool Docks; at the height of operations some 2,000 wagons were shunted daily by gravity in the yard.

Above **LIVERPOOL EDGE HILL STATION**

Another picture taken from Picton Road bridge on the same day, but looking in the opposite direction towards Edge Hill station. On the right are Edge Hill goods station and the running lines to Waterloo goods station for the docks. Seen on the left above the signal are the Down sidings, Edge Hill carriage sidings and the lines to Park Lane goods station. 'Jubilee' no. 45681 *Aboukir* passes through with the 11.05 express to Euston, taking the Up fast line; Edge Hill No. 2 signal box is seen in the centre.

Above LIVERPOOL LIME STREET STATION

Edge Hill had been the location for the original terminus of the Liverpool & Manchester Railway, which was the first all-steam line (no horses) in Britain. Soon a site in the centre of Liverpool was deemed desirable and the extension was begun in 1832, being ready for passengers in 1836. With the continued growth of the railways through the following decades, Liverpool Lime Street station was rebuilt in the late 1840s and again in the late 1860s. In the latter instance a single-span train shed was erected to the design of LNWR engineers W. Baker and F. Stevenson and was 219 ft wide, supported by cast-iron columns. In the 1870s a similar structure was erected along the southern side of the train shed and both have continued in use — having undergone refurbishments and alterations in the 20th and 21st centuries — to the present time. Pictured here in the northern half of Liverpool Lime Street at platform 6 with the 10.05 express to Bournemouth West on 13th June 1959 is Fowler 'Patriot' Class no. 45515 *Caernarvon*.

Below

LIVERPOOL LIME STREET STATION

The cavernous train shed at Liverpool Lime Street station also features in this photograph, taken on 10th June 1959. Stanier 'Jubilee' Class 4-6-0 no. 45670 *Howard of Effingham* stands at platform 7 with the 10.05 express destined for Birmingham New Street station. The locomotive entered traffic to Crewe North shed in December 1935, but had several moves subsequently and by the end of 1958 was allocated to Longsight shed, residing there until September 1960 when transferred to Llandudno. Withdrawal from Warrington occurred in November 1963.

Below

LIVERPOOL SPEKE JUNCTION SHED

Forty additional Hughes 'Crab' Class 2-6-0s were required when Stanier took over and he decided to modify the design. Mainly these alterations included replacing the parallel boiler with a taper boiler, which was pressed to 225 lb per sq. in., and the cylinders were reduced in size to 18 in. by 28 in. stroke; the increase in boiler pressure offset the loss of cylinder diameter. The locomotives were built at Crewe Works between 1933 and 1934, with no. 2946 being the second to be turned out (as no. 13246) in November 1933. From the mid-1930s to the early 1940s the engine was predominantly allocated to Workington depot and after three years at Crewe South shed from 1942, no. 2946 began a four-year stint at Speke Junction shed, Liverpool. The engine is pictured there on 20th June 1948 with an LMSR-style smokebox numberplate and 'LMS' still applied to the tender — this is just visible through the large cloud of steam being emitted from the cab area.

Above LLANDUDNO JUNCTION STATION

View west to Llandudno Junction station from the connecting bridge from Queen's Road to River View Terrace, 7th September 1962. The Chester & Holyhead Railway passed Llandudno to the south when opened, but the growth of the town over the following decade necessitated the construction of a branch line. This left the main route just before the line crossed the River Conway and headed north. A station — Llandudno Junction — was provided upon opening on 1st October 1858 and this subsequently served the Conway & Llanrwst Railway's line between the two places; later an extension took the route to Blaenau Ffestiniog. Before the turn of the century Llandudno Junction was replaced by a new station to the east which had improved facilities to deal with the traffic on the three lines. Nuneaton's Stanier 8F no. 48289 takes the Chester-line out of the station with an Up freight; the Blaenau Ffestiniog route is seen on the extreme left, while the Llandudno line was on the opposite side of the station.

Above LONDON CRICKLEWOOD STATION

The MR ran London trains via the London & Birmingham Railway route at first, then switched to the Great Northern Railway for a time before the company constructed a new line between Bedford and London St Pancras. This opened in 1868 but two years elapsed before Cricklewood was provided with a station, the title of which gave precedence to the nearby Childs Hill — a situation which persisted until just after the turn of the century. The station is the location for this image, taken on 18th June 1948, featuring Ivatt 2MT 2-6-2T locomotive no. 1207 at the head of a local service from St Pancras to St Albans. A recent addition to stock (December 1946), the engine would continue in service until November 1966.

Opposite above LONDON CRICKLEWOOD STATION

This Johnson 2441 Class 0-6-0T began life as MR no. 2444 in July 1901, having been erected by Vulcan Foundry. In the 1907 renumbering scheme the engine took no. 1903 and during the 1930s was altered again to no. 7203 which is still visible on the engine nearly seven months after Nationalisation. With 'British Railways' being applied to the tank sides, the locomotive must have been in works very early on in 1948 to receive this and the 'M' prefix briefly used after the switchover before the number prefixes were adopted. No. M7203 is seen at London Cricklewood with a mixed freight train.

Opposite below LONDON CRICKLEWOOD STATION

'Patriot' Class no. 45536 *Private W. Wood, V.C.* rushes through Cricklewood station with the 07.25 from Manchester Central station. The locomotive was constructed in May 1933, but was later rebuilt with a new boiler in November 1948. The photograph was taken on 6th May 1961, which was 18 months before the engine would be withdrawn, and at this time no. 45536 was allocated Sheffield Millhouses shed, being one of only two class members based there during the BR period. The locomotive spent the last year in service working from two other depots in the Rotherham/Sheffield area — Canklow and Darnall (six months at each).

Above **LONDON LITTLE OXHEY LANE BRIDGE**

Rural scenes either side of the WCML north of Hatch End near Little Oxhey Lane bridge are the first signs for the passengers of the 15.45 express from Euston to Manchester London Road that they are approaching the limit of the London Suburbs on 13th July 1957. Stanier 'Jubilee' no. 45674 *Duncan* is at the head of the train.

Opposite above **LONDON EUSTON STATION**

View north at London Euston station from platforms 15 and 14 (on the far west side) on 6th April 1962. Fowler 4P Class 2-6-4T no. 42367 has brought a train of empty stock from Willesden carriage sidings for a Down express. The train shed had not yet been lost to the major reconstruction work outlined by BR's Modernisation Plan as part of the WCML electrification. Euston had been under threat of redevelopment from the 1930s as the LMSR found the capacity inadequate but conditions were not conducive to a project of this size being started. In the late 1950s LMR architect R.L. Moorcroft in partnership with Richard Seifert & Partners planned the new station and Taylor Woodrow Construction was awarded the contract for the work in 1961; demolition began the following year. The first job saw the iconic portico entrance to the station demolished and subsequently moved on to the train shed and platforms: the whole project was not completed until 1968.

Opposite below **LONDON EUSTON STATION**

Stanier 'Coronation' Class Pacific no. 46228 *Duchess of Rutland* prepares to depart from platform 13 with the 10.25 express to Carlisle and Windermere. In the background is Ampthill Bridge No. 2 which was demolished during the modernisation; Ampthill Bridge No. 1 had been pulled down during a major resignalling in 1952.

LONDON MARYLEBONE STATION

The 1948 Locomotive Exchanges were conducted on all regions involving the three main types of locomotive: passenger, mixed traffic and freight. Representing the LMR in the second-mentioned category on the London Marylebone to Manchester route was Class 5 no. 45253, which is seen here entering the former station on 16th June 1948.

Above **LONDON QUEENS PARK STATION**

Johnson 0-6-0 no. 3561 travels west towards Willesden carriage sidings with a rake of empty carriages. Seen just east of London Queens Park station on 24th April 1948, the engine would be withdrawn from Rugby in 1954.

Below **LONDON ST PANCRAS STATION**

W.H. Barlow was the architect for London St Pancras station and one of the main features was the single-span roof, measuring 245 ft across. Accommodated underneath is 'Jubilee' Class no. 45614 *Leeward Islands*, which is at the head of an express on 18th March 1961.

Above **LONDON ST PANCRAS STATION**

The BR Standard Class 5 was from a similar mould to Stanier's design for the LMSR and was produced in relatively large numbers between 1951 and 1957 at Derby and Doncaster Works. Thirty were fitted with British-Caprotti rotary-cam valve gear and poppet valves following experiments conducted by the LMSR before Nationalisation. No. 73142 was fitted with the valves and valve gear at Derby, being ready for service in December 1956 and allocated to Leicester. The engine is only six months old here, but looks older, and is seen waiting to leave London St Pancras station with the 10.50 to Leicester.

Opposite above **LONDON ST PANCRAS STATION**

These two Stanier 3P Class 2-6-2T locomotives, nos 160 and M161, were completed within days of each other at Derby Works in late October and early November 1937 respectively. The pair are reunited at London St Pancras station on 10th June 1948 while engaged on empty stock work, both being allocated to Kentish Town shed at the time. Nos 160 and M161 would be condemned there in 1959 and 1960.

Opposite below **LONDON WEMBLEY CENTRAL STATION**

The 5th May 1962 was FA Cup Final day and saw Burnley take on Tottenham Hotspur at Wembley Stadium. Many fans from the north were brought to the capital by rail and one of the trains is seen here at Wembley Central station. Two Stanier Class 5s have transported the supporters from Colne via Stockport; leading is no. 45229 and trailing is no. 44940, both being allocated to Rose Grove shed.

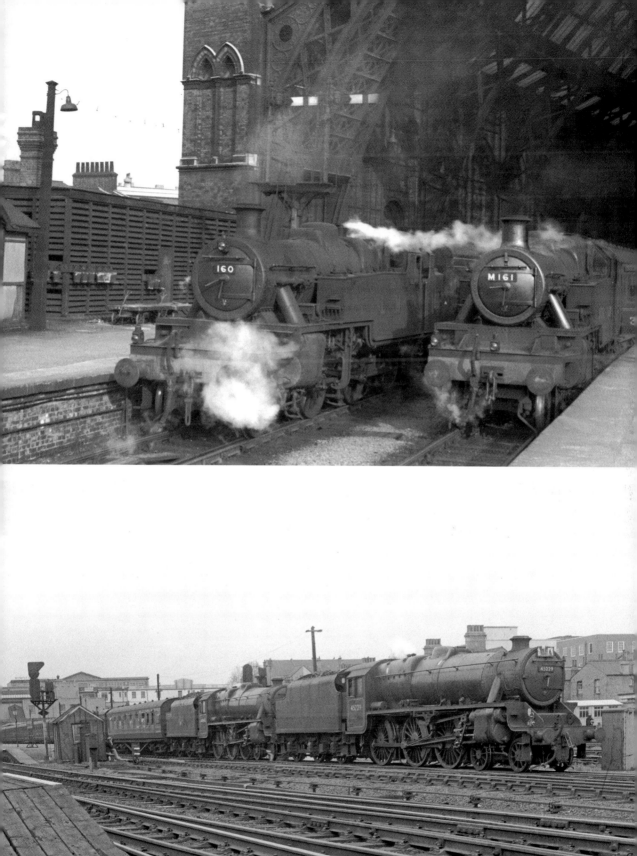

LONDON WEMBLEY CENTRAL STATION

Stanier Class 4MT 2-6-4T no. 42470 approaches Wembley Central station from the south with a local service on 4th May 1962. Opened by the London & Birmingham Railway on 8th August 1842, the station was originally called Sudbury and this remained in sole use for forty years before Wembley was added. This took prominence in the early 20th century and after Nationalisation Wembley Central became the title.

Above **LONDON WEMBLEY CENTRAL STATION**

Another fan special for the 1962 FA Cup Final has been conveyed to Wembley by a Lancashire-based engine. Stanier 'Jubilee' Class no. 45705 *Seahorse* was allocated to Blackpool shed at this time and had been there from July 1956 following 20 years in Yorkshire at Farnley Junction. The locomotive arrived there new from Crewe Works in May 1936 along with three other classmates constructed at the same time. These were amongst the first of the class to be fitted with an improved boiler tube arrangement after steaming troubles had been encountered by previous engines. Leaving Blackpool for Newton Heath in June 1964, *Seahorse* was withdrawn from there in November 1965.

Above LONDON WILLESDEN JUNCTION STATION

Stanier 'Jubilee' no. 45704 *Leviathan* was completed several days before no. 45705 *Seahorse*, which is seen on the previous page, and spent a similar period employed at Farnley Junction shed. The engine left for Carlisle Kingmoor in September 1952 and had several years there before a restless period between 1959 and 1960 when six moves were undertaken. *Leviathan* drifted between Crewe, Liverpool, Llandudno, Camden, Aston and Willesden before settling at Rugby in January 1961. No. 45704 is seen here reversing down the Up main platform line at Willesden Junction station on 5th May 1962. The engine spent 18 months at Crewe North shed from June 1963 and was then condemned for scrap.

Opposite LONDON WILLESDEN JUNCTION STATION

No. 42234 — a Fairburn variant of Stanier's 2-6-4T design — was built in July 1946 and spent many of the ensuing years working the North Stafford local services. Before withdrawal in February 1964 , the locomotive had a spell at London Willesden shed and is pictured at Willesden Junction station with an empty stock working. The station was the centre for several lines but this was not the case when the London & Birmingham Railway built the facilities in 1841 and in 1866 a new station was erected to take advantage. There were connections with the North London Line, the West London line — both of which passed above (a glimmer of the High Level station building is seen above the locomotive's cab and the first carriage) — and the London & South Western Junction Railway line. In 1912 further platforms were added for use by Euston-Watford electric trains, and later by Bakerloo line services (on the right).

Above LOUGHBOROUGH

Loughborough was served by two main lines for more than 60 years. The first was the Midland following the merger of the NMR, B&DJR and MCR, the latter having opened Loughborough station in 1840. In the late 1890s the GCR built Loughborough Central on the London Extension which remained in use until the mid-1960s. Here, on 6th October 1950, the two lines are seen, with the GCR route running over the MR main line. No. 58298 (Johnson/Deeley 2F Class 0-6-0) has an Up local goods heading to Leicester on the latter, while an O4/1 (Robinson 2-8-0) travels northward on the former with a Down empties train. The GCR section of track between Leicester, Loughborough and Ruddington has subsequently been reopened as a heritage railway, but operates in two sections as the bridge seen in the picture was removed in the 1980s. There are plans to restore this (and others) to join the two parts together, creating an unbroken line 18 miles long.

Opposite above LONDON WILLESDEN JUNCTION STATION

An Up freight trundles through Willesden Junction station on 25th August 1962 with no. 46431. The locomotive was built to H.G. Ivatt's design based on his Class 2MT and was completed at Crewe in December 1948. From November 1958 to May 1963 no. 46431 was allocated to Watford shed.

Opposite below LOSTOCK HALL SHED

View from Watkin Lane, Lostock Hall, to the locomotive shed on 20th August 1963. Despite appearances, the site had not been abandoned and would remain in use right up to the death throes of steam in August 1968. Originally, the Preston & Blackburn Railway established modest servicing facilities to the east of Lostock Hall station but after these became outdated (and the company had been absorbed by the Lancashire & Yorkshire Railway) a large eight-road depot was built in 1881 on the south side of the line to Preston directly opposite the station. A trio of 3F 0-6-0T locomotives stand on the south side of the depot, the closest pair being, from front to rear, no. 47360 and no. 47211 and on the far side no. 47201. The latter two were built by the MR in August 1899 and June 1901 respectively and no. 47360 dated from 1926. Despite being the youngest, the latter had been withdrawn a month earlier, yet no. 47211 would continue to November 1964 and no. 47201 December 1966; all three spent relatively brief periods at Lostock Hall shed. After closure to steam the depot remained in railway use until the late 1980s, then being demolished and the site sits unoccupied at present.

Above **MADELEY STATION**

Located on the main line between Stafford and Crewe, Madeley station was opened by the Grand Junction Railway on 4th July 1837, later closing on 4th February 1952. Passing through the remains of the station on 19th April 1962 is 'Crab' Class 2-6-0 no. 42852 which is heading a train of smart-looking carriages northward.

Opposite above **LOUGHBOROUGH**

Several designers developed articulated steam locomotives over the years, one of the most famous being H.W. Garratt. His design, which saw the locomotive split into three separate parts, was marketed by Beyer, Peacock & Co. and many examples were constructed subsequently. However, in Britain the Beyer Garratt locomotive was not particularly suited to the network and received little attention from locomotive engineers. The only real exception was made by the LMSR which ordered three shortly after Grouping to remove the need for double heading heavy coal trains between the Midlands and London and these entered service in 1927. No. 47999 was the last of the first batch to be completed in April 1927 as no. 4999, being renumbered in November 1939. The locomotive has been pictured on 6th October 1950 alongside the Midland main line at Loughborough (to the east of the station) with a short coal train. Allocated to Toton at this time (in fact from the early 1940s), the engine was withdrawn from there in January 1956. Interestingly, no. 47999 was one of only two LMSR Beyer Garratts, which totalled 33, not fitted with a rotary coal bunker in the early 1930s.

Opposite below **MADELEY**

The presence of Standard Class Pacific no. 70032 *Tennyson*, which is whistling past on the Up Fast line at Madeley on 19th April 1962, does nothing to disturb the hard-earned tea break of this engineering gang.

Above MANCHESTER EXCHANGE STATION

Manchester Exchange was another station built due to the poor relations between railway companies and lack of space in a shared facility. The LNWR inherited a position in the L&YR-owned Manchester Victoria in the late 1840s but as the 1880s began plans were formulated for a new station to be constructed. This was completed in 1885 and located only a short distance to the south west of Manchester Victoria, being built with five platforms on arches spanning the River Irwell. After Grouping the two stations were linked following the extension of platform 11 at Victoria to platform 3 at Exchange, but the two still remained largely independent. Following the rationalisations of the network in the 1960s, Exchange station was set for closure, which occurred on 5th May 1969, and the site has since been cleared for redevelopment. This event was still some time away when BR Standard Class 5 no. 73163 was pictured pulling up to the station's platform 4 with a train of empty carriages on 3rd September 1960. The locomotive was constructed at Doncaster Works in February 1957 and was in service for just eight years; at this time no. 73163 was based at Huddersfield shed.

Opposite MANCHESTER EXCHANGE STATION

Pictured not once but twice at Manchester Exchange station on 27th July 1966 is BR Standard Class 5 4-6-0 no. 73144. In the first scene the locomotive arrives from the south west with a short pick-up freight train, whilst in the second no. 73144 has stopped at platform 3 — perhaps to collect, given the abundance of goods trolleys on the platform. The engine was one of 30 class members fitted with British Caprotti valve gear and was sent into traffic from Derby during December 1956. Allocated to Leicester Midland depot from then until March 1958, no. 73144 subsequently worked from Nottingham, Derby, Rowsley and finally Patricroft before withdrawal in August 1967.

Below

MANCHESTER NEWTON HEATH STATION

Whilst the primary role of Stanier's 8F design was the haulage of freight and mineral trains, the class were no strangers to the occasional passenger service, performing well on these given their ample power, although there was no connection to provide steam for the heating system in the carriages. This was not a concern with the stock seen running behind no. 48631 as the coaches were empty. Heading westward through Newton Heath station on 18th April 1962, the engine still had nearly six years left in service before withdrawal, but the station would be taken out of use first at the start of 1966.

Above **MANCHESTER PICCADILLY STATION**

Another project undertaken as part of the WCML electrification was the modernisation of facilities at Manchester London Road station, which was renamed Manchester Piccadilly in the middle of the work in 1960. The eastern side is seen here from the footbridge connecting the main building with the platforms for the Manchester, South Junction & Altrincham Railway suburban line to Hale off to the right and undergoing renewal and lengthening at this time. In the distance is the LNWR No. 2 signal box, which is still protected by a steel canopy installed during the war and on the left is the ex-LNER signal box and the electrified lines for the Woodhead route. The station was opened by the Manchester & Birmingham Railway in partnership with the Sheffield, Ashton-under-Lyne & Manchester Railway during 1842 as Manchester Store Street, being renamed Manchester London Road in 1847. Only 20 years after opening the station had become too small for the two companies and was reconstructed, with the MS&LR taking the north half and the LNWR the southern — a division which remained well into the BR era. Arriving at platform 5 with the 11.50 express from Swansea via Hereford, Shrewsbury and Crewe on 9th June 1959 is Stanier Class 5 no. 44835.

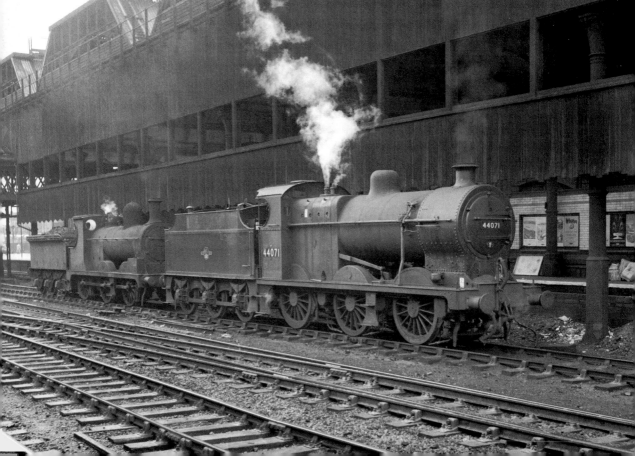

Above MANCHESTER VICTORIA STATION

Class 5 no. 44751 has just descended Miles Platting bank with a diverted express on 3rd September 1960 and approaches the long through platform 11 at Manchester Victoria. As London Road was undergoing major engineering work many expresses (36 over nearly 3 hours — 26 headed by Class 5s — which was surely a treat for these enthusiasts) were sent via Ardwick Junction to Victoria.

Opposite above MANCHESTER VICTORIA STATION

Ivatt's Class 4MT 2-6-0 was the successor to the 4F and a total of 162 were erected up to 1952, with 75 emerging from Horwich, 50 from Doncaster and 37 at Darlington. This picture — taken at Manchester Victoria station on 19th June 1948 — is perhaps one of the first of no. 43019 as the engine had only been completed at Horwich a few days earlier. Derby shed was to receive the engine following running in (a shed plate is yet to be fitted), but the locomotive was there only six months before moving to Saltley. After a year there, and nearly three years at Nottingham, no. 43019 was transferred to Cricklewood where a decade was spent working in the area. Wellingborough, Stoke, Lower Darwen and Lostock Hall depots all accommodated the engine for at least a year before withdrawal occurred in May 1968.

Opposite below MANCHESTER VICTORIA STATION

Trains heading north east out of Manchester Victoria had the formidable Miles Platting bank, with gradients of 1 in 59 and 1 in 47 for approx 1.5 miles, to contend with almost immediately. Bankers often had to be provided and two are seen here at the station on 3rd September 1960 waiting to be called into action. Fowler 4F no. 44071 is prominent and behind stands Aspinall 27 Class 0-6-0 no. 52270.

Above MANCHESTER VICTORIA STATION

The Aspinall 3F (L&YR Class 27) locomotive seen with the 4F on the previous page has assisted a train up Miles Platting bank and has returned to the station for the next run. The Class 27 0-6-0s were the standard goods locomotive on the railway and nearly 500 were erected between 1889 and 1918, with no. 52270 completed at Horwich in December 1894 and remaining in traffic until January 1961.

Opposite above MANCHESTER VICTORIA STATION

The dirty and decaying train shed at Manchester Victoria contrasts sharply with two new skyscrapers built in the city during the early 1960s. The pair, which have recently been refurbished, are the CIS Tower (tallest) and New Century House, built for the Co-operative Society to the designs of G.S. Hay and G. Tait (both buildings). Fairburn 2-6-4T no. 42696 is the focus of this picture taken on 24th August 1963 and shows the engine shunting wagons as part of the station pilot duty that the locomotive had been assigned. No. 42696 was erected at Derby Works in October 1945 and subsequently worked in Scotland until 1960, when returning to England and allocated to Newton Heath depot. The locomotive was condemned there in August 1964.

Opposite below MANCHESTER NEWTON HEATH

Newton Heath (north east from Manchester city centre) was a major centre for the Lancashire & Yorkshire Railway. A large area on the north side of the main line was occupied by Carriage and Wagons Works, Carriage Sidings and a Locomotive Shed. Stanier 2-6-4T no. 42607 is seen here on 18th April 1962 in the Carriage Sidings collecting a train — perhaps a local service to Wigan as this was the engine's base at the time. The locomotive was built by the NBLC in December 1936 and was in service until February 1964.

Above **MARSDEN**

Class 5 no. 45063 has just completed the 10-mile climb to Marsden on the Leeds-Manchester line and prepares to enter the 3-mile long Standege Tunnel on 11th April 1960. The train is the 16.00 from Hull to Liverpool Lime Street via Manchester Exchange station.

Opposite above **MARKET HARBOROUGH**

A total of 935 War Department 'Austerity' Class 2-8-0s were constructed during the war. The NBLC produced the largest number — 545 — while the Vulcan Foundry erected the remaining 390. As the latter built the final 'Austerity' locomotive in May 1945 (as WD no. 79312) the engine was named after the works. Subsequently transported to France, the locomotive was employed there until 1947 when repatriated and loaned to the LNER in November 1947, being allocated to March shed. Renumbered 90732 in May 1950, *Vulcan* was housed at Colchester, Doncaster and Frodingham before withdrawal in September 1962. The engine was three years from this event when photographed at Market Harborough in October 1959.

Opposite below **MARKET HARBOROUGH STATION**

Johnson 3F (MR 1798) Class 0-6-0 no. 43261 shunts an assorted train of wagons at Market Harborough station on 30th October 1957. The engine was condemned in early 1962.

Above **MATLOCK STATION**

View south east at Matlock station as Hughes 6P5F 'Crab' Class 2-6-0 no. 42873 heads a freight train northward towards Manchester on 23rd June 1961. The station was opened on 4th June 1849 by the Manchester, Buxton, Matlock & Midland Junction Railway which intended to connect the LNWR line at Buxton with the NMR route just north of Derby, but only reached Rowsley at the time. Since 1968 Matlock has been the terminus for the southern portion of the line, but part of the closed section has been resurrected as a heritage route by Peak Rail, with services running into the station.

Opposite above **MILFORD**

Johnson 3F (MR 1698) Class 0-6-0 no. 43185 was built at Derby Works in December 1887 towards the end of the construction run for the class, which had begun in February 1885. Originally numbered 1793, the change to 3185 occurred in September 1907 and BR's '4' prefix was added during 1948. Between the engine entering traffic and withdrawal in August 1961, the locomotive was rebuilt twice. In the first instance an H-type boiler was was fitted at the end of 1904 and this was in turn replaced by the G7-type in early 1925. No. 43185 is seen shortly after exiting Milford Tunnel (just north of Duffield on the ex-North Midland Railway line) on 15th June 1957.

Opposite below **MILFORD**

Also pictured at Milford was Stanier 4P Class 2-6-4T no. 42431, which hauls the 13.20 local train from Darley Dale to Derby. The 4P Class were introduced in 1934 to work traffic on the Southend line to tight schedules. Three cylinders were fitted for quick acceleration after the many service stops, although in practice this did not provide a distinct advantage. A total of 37 were built at Derby, but subsequent engines were constructed with just two cylinders and several batches were completed between 1935 and 1943 at Derby and the NBLC. No. 42431 was erected at Derby in March 1936 and was in service until May 1966. In June 1957 the engine was nearing the end of an allocation to Stoke shed and would move on to Chester in October.

Above **MIRFIELD**

The Manchester & Leeds Railway skirted the southern edge of Mirfield when the first section opened in 1840, but not until mid-1845 did a station open to serve the town and this was later upgraded in 1866. Running on the line west of the station with an eastbound empties train is Fowler 7F Class 0-8-0 no. 49561. The class, which ultimately totalled 175, was introduced in 1929 as an improvement on the LNWR 0-8-0s then in service and no. 49561 was erected at Crewe Works in September 1929, remaining in traffic until June 1950; this was only two months away when the locomotive was photographed.

Opposite above **MILLBROOK**

Doncaster-built Stanier 8F no. 48510 travels northward with a freight train at Millbrook (north of Ampthill on the Midland main line) on 30th April 1960. The locomotive was the first of the LNER-ordered 8Fs to be completed at Doncaster Works in June 1943, being classified O6 by the company. No. 48510 was initially allocated to Tyne Dock shed, then Heaton, working on the important wartime freight trains. In June 1947 the engine was transferred to the LMSR and was based at Wakefield and Mirfield before relocating to Liverpool. After stints at several sheds in the area, no. 48510 began work at Derby in October 1953 and remained employed there until January 1966 when moved to Colwick. At the end of the year Lostock Hall depot took the locomotive on and withdrawal occurred from there in January 1968.

Opposite below **MILLERS DALE**

During the early 1860s, the MR finally extended the Ambergate to Rowsley line to meet the LNWR route into Manchester at Buxton. One of the new stations on the section was Millers Dale which opened on 1st June 1863. As traffic on the line increased, so did the importance of Millers Dale as an interchange for places in the area, such as Tideswell, which was added to the title in May 1889, and Buxton. By the turn of the century the volume of traffic necessitated a new island platform and viaduct to be built at the east end of the station. Millers Dale would continue to be busy until closure on 6th March 1967. On 14th June 1957 Fowler 4F Class 0-6-0 no. 44602 advances from the west with a mixed freight train.

Above **MIRFIELD SHED**

Two Stanier 8Fs — no. 48146 in the foreground and no. 48095 behind — pass Mirfield shed, which was located to the west of the station, with freight trains on 24th June 1964.

Opposite above **MIRFIELD STATION**

The 10.30 Liverpool Exchange to York express speeds through Mirfield station on 8th July 1961. In charge of the train is Stanier 'Jubilee' Class 4-6-0 no. 45698 *Mars*. Note the colour-light signals installed by the LMSR in 1932 to improve traffic flow on this busy section of the network.

Opposite below **MIRFIELD STATION**

Returning empty coal wagons to one of the many Yorkshire collieries is Stanier 8F no. 48676. The engine, which is pictured at Mirfield station on 29th July 1966, was built at Brighton Works in April 1944 and survived until October 1967. For many years no. 48676 was allocated to Heaton Mersey shed, but was working from Aintree here.

Above NORTHWICH SHED

View from Middlewich Road, Northwich, to the locomotive shed's turntable on 12th April 1966, featuring Stanier 8F no. 48766 of Stoke. The facilities were opened by the Cheshire Lines Committee in the late 1860s after two lines serving Northwich had been opened and absorbed. The shed, which was located just to the east of the station, originally comprised two tracks, but was later extended to four roads. The shed remained open to steam until early 1968, when turned over to diesels and remained engaged in this role until the 1980s, subsequently being demolished.

Opposite above MORECAMBE (PROMENADE) STATION

Morecambe (Promenade) station was an early 20th century replacement for Morecambe Northumberland Street station which had been opened in 1848 as part of the 'Little' North Western Railway's line between Skipton-Lancaster-Morecambe. Interestingly, the new station was part of early MR experiments with electrification (using a 6,600V system) and this remained in almost constant use until the mid-1960s. Here, on 8th June 1959, steam power in the form of Fairburn 2-6-4T no. 42135 is favoured for the 14.15 service to Crewe.

Opposite below NANTWICH STATION

An unidentified bank holiday special pauses at Nantwich station on 6th August 1962. The station — opened by the LNWR in 1858 — served two routes, the main one being the Crewe to Shrewsbury line, while the other was the GWR's line to Market Drayton and Wellington. The locomotive is Stanier 4P Class 2-6-4T no. 42575.

Above NOTTINGHAM, BESTWOOD ROAD

View south from the same spot on Bestwood Road, Nottingham as the picture opposite below. Another 8F — no. 48214 — has been engaged on a coal train working and in this instance is returning empty wagons to Bestwood Colliery Sidings. The viaduct prominent in the background carried the GCR main line and was erected in an impressively short time of just over 12 months in the 1890s. The structure spanned some 420 yards at an average height of 44 ft with a total of 26 arches; the whole endeavour consumed over 6.5 million bricks.

Opposite above NOTTINGHAM BASFORD NORTH STATION

By the 1860s the MR had a stranglehold of coal traffic emanating from the collieries in the Nottingham and Derby areas and set prices accordingly to benefit the company. The GNR was given concessions to break this monopoly and construct a line from Grantham through to Nottingham, Derby and Burton-on-Trent. One of the stations opened for passengers on completion in the mid-1870s was Basford North which is just visible behind Ivatt Class 4MT 2-6-0 no. 43059. The engine is making one of several stops with the 17.18 Nottingham Victoria to Derby Friargate station on 21st August 1963. The locomotive was erected at Doncaster in October 1950 and was initially allocated to Peterborough New England. After eight years there a move to Boston occurred, followed by a switch to Colwick in January 1963. No. 43059 would reside at Barrow Hill shed from July 1964 until condemned in January 1965. Basford North station had been closed several months earlier in September 1964.

Opposite below NOTTINGHAM, BESTWOOD ROAD

This scene, showing Stanier 8F no. 48395 travelling south on 12th July 1963, was captured from Bestwood Road, Bulwell Forest, Nottingham. No. 48395 has collected a loaded train of coal wagons from Bestwood Colliery Sidings and is perhaps taking them to one of the large yards at Toton or Colwick for distribution further afield. The engine was allocated to Kirkby-in-Ashfield at this time and would be based there for a total of 11 years from 1954 to 1967, having a spell away at Toton from late 1956 to mid-1958. Withdrawal from Edge Hill depot occurred in September 1967 after 22 years in traffic.

Above **NOTTINGHAM VICTORIA STATION**

Drawing up to platform 4 at Nottingham Victoria is Stanier 'Jubilee' Class 4-6-0 no. 45638 *Zanzibar*. The locomotive is seen with the 08.38 express from London Marylebone station on 12th October 1962; a Thompson L1 Class 2-6-4T loiters on the middle road. The station was opened on 24th May 1900 and saw the last London express in September 1966, with local services ending the following year. Demolition followed swiftly and a shopping centre was erected on the site.

Opposite above **NOTTINGHAM VICTORIA STATION**

Around Nationalisation, improved timings were made to the freight services running on the ex-GCR line between the freight yards at Annesley (north of Nottingham) and Woodford Halse (south of Rugby). The crews in charge of these heavy loose-coupled freight and mineral trains were expected to complete the undulating 65 miles in just over 3½ hours and often prevailed, earning the trains the sobriquet 'Wind Cutters' or 'Runners'. A northbound service nears the end of the journey on 12th October 1962, passing through Nottingham Victoria station behind BR Standard Class 9F 2-10-0 no. 92011. A large number of Doncaster's 9Fs had been reallocated to Annesley in 1957 to replace Thompson O1s and Robinson O4s that were previously used, but no. 92011 left Peterborough New England at the same time to join the ranks at Annesley. Also in the picture is English-Electric Type 3 diesel D6753 which is just departing with the 10.08 York to Bournemouth express.

Opposite below **NOTTINGHAM VICTORIA STATION**

The south end of Nottingham Victoria station was spanned by a footbridge connecting the platforms and a wide road bridge carrying Lower Parliament Street to Upper Parliament Street. Controlling the movements at this end of the station was Nottingham Victoria South signal box which sits in the shadow of the road bridge. Stanier Class 5 no. 44912 waits for the road on 14th March 1959 with with a Sheffield Victoria to Poole express.

Above PETERBOROUGH

Peterborough was an important place for the interchange of freight and passengers. The LNWR and MR both operated passenger services to Peterborough East station, where their engine sheds serviced and housed locomotives, some of which were used for shunting and local work. Here, Fowler 3F Class 0-6-0T no. 43700 of Peterborough Spital Bridge shed is engaged on a Down pick-up freight service on 15th August 1959, running on the ex-MR Syston-Peterborough line at Walton (just north of the city).

Opposite above NUNEATON SHED

The use of compound cylinder systems was attempted only sporadically in Britain. These often found only very limited success despite much being achieved on the continent and elsewhere. On the LNWR, F.W. Webb produced several compound types, one being the Class A 0-8-0s which appeared in traffic during the final years of the 19th century. No. 49047 — the front end of which is seen here at Nuneaton shed on 15th March 1953 — was one such locomotive, constructed at Crewe in October 1897 as no. 1808. The Class were not successful and Whale's successor C. Bowen Cooke rebuilt the whole class, but using two specifications. Latterly, a larger boiler was installed, along with simple cylinders, and no. 1808 was so fitted in mid-1908. The locomotive was later rebuilt twice by the LMSR, finally becoming a G1 Class engine and in this form no. 49047 was condemned at Stafford in January 1958. Interestingly, the class (known as 'Super D's') were never fitted with smokebox number plates and the reason for this has not been established.

Opposite below NUNEATON SHED

Also 'on shed' at Nuneaton (being visible in the background to the right of no. 49047 seen opposite above) was ex-MR Johnson 1698 Class 0-6-0 no. 58240. The locomotive was constructed at Derby Works in March 1887 as no. 1769, subsequently becoming no. 3161 in 1907. Based at Nuneaton when pictured the locomotive would be condemned there only two months later in May 1953. Nuneaton shed was located south of the station in between the junction for the main line to Rugby and the route to Coventry. Erected by the LNWR in the late 1870s, the depot remained operational until mid-1966.

Above **PRESTON STATION**

View looking north, over platform 6, from the south end footbridge at Preston station on 29th July 1950, with the carriage sidings on the east side of the station to the right. Coming off platform 7 is Stanier Class 5 no. 45244 with the 13.10 from Workington to Manchester. The engine was a long-term resident at Carlisle Upperby shed during the BR period and only moved twice shortly before withdrawal in August 1963 to Wigan and Edge Hill depots.

Opposite above **PETERBOROUGH**

Fowler 4F 0-6-0 no. 44178 heads the 10.37 Yarmouth Vauxhall to Leicester London Road express at Walton, just north of Peterborough, on 15th August 1959. The locomotive was erected at St Rollox Works in December 1924 as one of thirty completed to Lot No. 11. Allocated to Toton between July 1958 and October 1963, withdrawal from Westhouses depot would occur in November 1964. The East Coast Main line can be seen running parallel to the ex-MR line on the left and in the distance is the Peter Brotherhood Ltd premises.

Opposite below **PETERBOROUGH**

The ex-MR line paralleled the ECML for approx. five miles from Werrington (a short distance north of Walton) through to Peterborough East station (just to the south of the River Nene), allowing a wide variety of locomotive types to be seen on this stretch. On this occasion Fowler 4F no. 43965 has been caught a little south of Walton station with the 12.42 stopping train from Leicester London Road to Peterborough East on 20th August 1949. One of twenty 4Fs built by Armstrong Whitworth & Co. in December 1921, the locomotive was renumbered in April 1949, yet still has 'LMS' applied to the tender. No. 43965 was allocated to Leicester at Nationalisation and transferred to Burton in October 1949, remaining there until May 1957. At this time the locomotive took up residence at Saltley and was condemned there in December 1959.

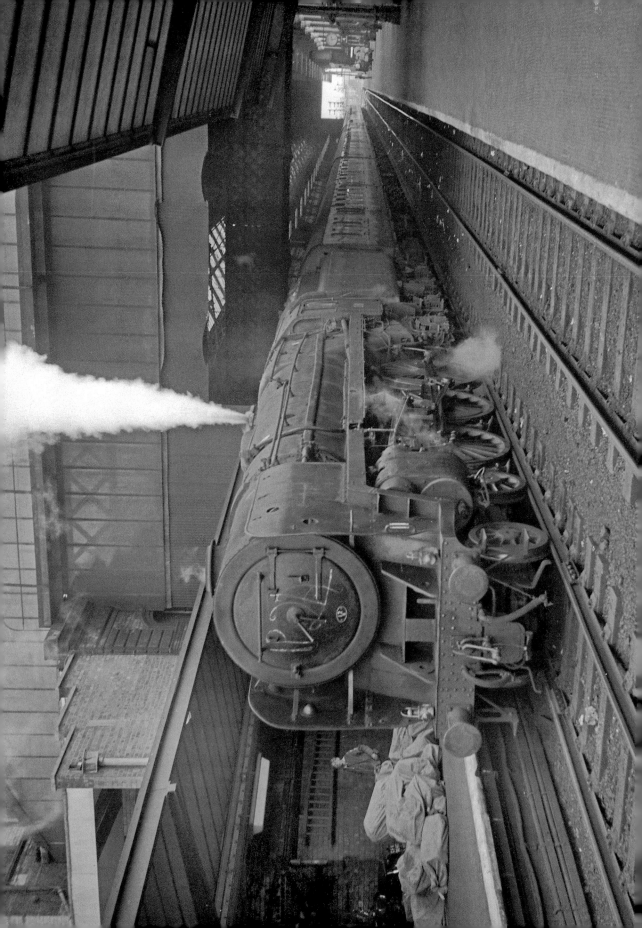

Above **PRESTON STATION**

Despite looking in 'fine fettle' Fowler 'Royal Scot' Class 4-6-0 no. 46105 *Cameron Highlander* was only three months away from being condemned for scrap when photographed on 8th September 1962 at Preston station with the 14.00 Manchester Victoria to Glasgow Central express. The locomotive was constructed by the NBLC in September 1927 and subsequently ran for just over 20 years before being rebuilt with a new boiler, amongst other components. *Cameron Highlander* was allocated to Glasgow Polmadie shed from 1943 until withdrawn.

Opposite **PRESTON STATION**

Thankfully the cabside number identifies this 'Britannia' Pacific as no. 70011. Built at Crewe Works in May 1951, the engine was named *Hotspur* after Sir Henry Percy, who had a distinguished military and diplomatic career under Richard II and Henry IV, later being immortalised in Shakespeare's *Henry IV, Part I*. Initially there had been no intention of naming the class, but upon advice the Railway Executive relented and ultimately chose a variety, with many celebrating famous British people as 1951 was the year of the Festival of Britain. No. 70011 managed to retain the nameplates until early 1964 when they were removed. *Hotspur* entered traffic to the Eastern Region at Norwich for the services to Liverpool Street and remained there until 1961 when moved to March. From 1963 until withdrawn in December 1967, the locomotive was allocated to one of the Carlisle sheds, mainly Kingmoor, with a spell at Upperby between February 1965 and December 1966. No. 70011 is pictured at Preston station on 23rd July 1966 with an express assembled from portions originating at Manchester Victoria and Liverpool Exchange and destined for Glasgow Central.

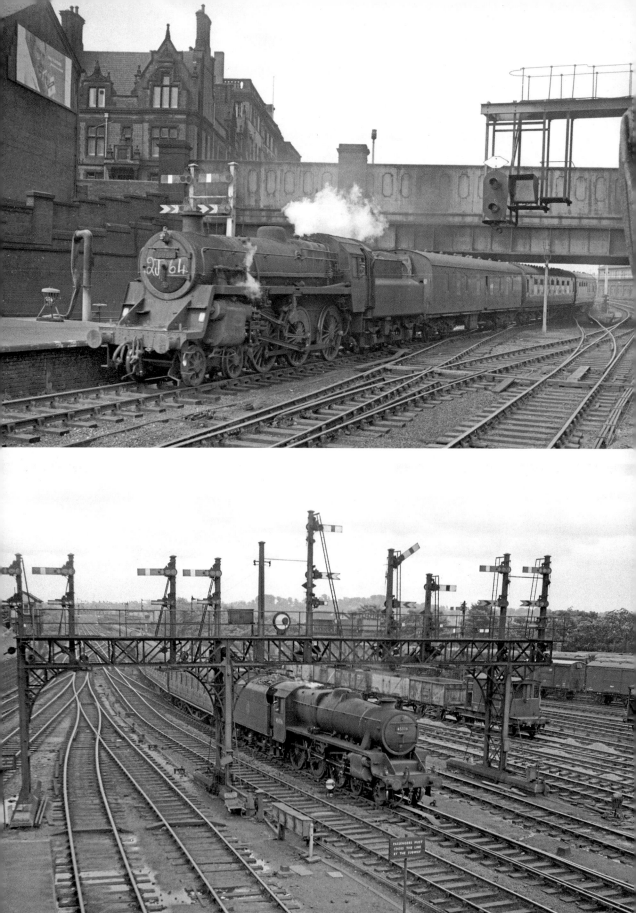

Above **PRESTON STATION**

Two Stanier locomotives get set to depart from the north end of Preston station on 17th August 1963. In the centre of the picture (at platform 4) is Class 4P 2-6-4T no. 42449 which has come on to the 13.20 train from Crewe to Windermere. On the left at platform 5 is Class 5 no. 45371 heading an unidentified express.

Opposite above **PRESTON STATION**

BR's Standard Class 4 4-6-0 design was introduced as a slightly smaller version of the Class 5 and intended for duties that the latter were precluded from through restrictions in axle load, etc. The main sphere of operation of the Class 4 was to be the WR, with the SR and ER also seen as having a need for the type. In the event, these regions only took on small numbers of the 80 that were erected and the majority spent their careers working on the LMR. No. 75046 was one of 20 built at Swindon Works between June and October 1953, entering service during the latter month to Accrington. After two years there the engine began the first of 11 years at Bank Hall depot, Liverpool. The locomotive is seen here arriving at Preston station (north end, under the Fishergate bridge) with the 13.35 stopping train from Blackpool to Manchester Victoria on 17th August 1963. After brief allocations to Heaton Mersey and Chester in early 1966, the locomotive spent a year at Croes Newydd before withdrawal from Stoke occurred in August 1967.

Opposite below **PRESTON STATION**

An impressive array of signals stand above the approach lines at the south end of Preston station and on the far right the lines to Preston Docks branch away. Under a caution signal is Stanier Class 5 no. 45336 which is leading the 16.20 from Manchester Victoria to Blackpool and Fleetwood on 8th June 1959.

Above **PRESTON STATION**

The Stanier Class 5 4-6-0s were undoubtedly an improvement on the LMSR stock in service when introduced. However, they were not without their own problems and a number of remedies were tried before these were finally overcome. One difficulty encountered was wear in the axleboxes which caused 'knocking', damage to the frames and rough riding. In the mid-1940s a small number of Class 5s were fitted with manganese steel axlebox liners and these increased the mileages between general repairs significantly. From April 1947 these became standard and no. 44769 (pictured), which was erected at Crewe Works during the same month, was an early recipient. The engine is seen at Preston station's platform 3 with the 13.20 Crewe-Windermere service on 17th August 1963, with the fireman perhaps checking the locomotive for any defects before departure.

Below **PRESTON STATION**

Fowler 'Patriot' Class 4-6-0 no. 45535 *Sir Herbert Walker, K.C.B.* creates interest for the local 'spotters' when passing through Preston station with an 'Illuminations' Special to Blackpool on 8th September 1962. The engine was erected at Derby Works in May 1933 as no. 5997, but remained unnamed until 1937 when taking that originally bestowed on no. 5529, which then went without a name until 1947. No. 45535 was rebuilt in September 1948 and was in traffic until October 1963.

Above **PRESTON STATION**

View north-west from East Cliff on the south east side of Preston station on 8th June 1959. The platforms in the middle distance are those used for the former East Lancashire Railway line from Blackburn and Liverpool and the West Lancashire Railway's route from Southport; both companies later fell to the L&YR. On the right is Butler Street goods depot, whilst in the background is the main station, opened in 1838 by the North Union Railway and subsequently rebuilt by the LNWR and L&YR, reopening in 1880. The locomotives visible in this picture are WD 'Austerity' no. 90266, a Stanier 2-6-4T (seen behind the former) and a Standard Class 2MT 2-6-0 (left). This area has since been occupied by a car park and shopping centre.

Opposite above **PRESTON STATION**

Stanier 'Jubilee' Class 4-6-0 no. 45679 *Armada* was one of a number of the class to be erected at Crewe Works in 1935 with a 4,000 gallon tender with curved top. At that time the 'Royal Scot' Class were experiencing excessive coal and water consumption and the intermediary measure of providing larger tenders for the class was approved. These were taken from a number of 'Jubilees' including no. 45679 which was relieved of tender no. 9150 and received Fowler-type tender no. 3927 from no. 6103 *Royal Scots Fusilier*. No. 45679 has a similar tender (perhaps not the original) trailing behind with the 10.40 from Blackpool North station to Manchester Victoria on 8th September 1962.

Opposite below **PRESTON**

Using a government loan, which was provided to help promote industrial recovery following the Depression, the LMSR placed an order with Armstrong Whitworth & Co. for 227 Stanier Class 5 locomotives. These were completed between August 1936 and December 1937, with no. 45448 (pictured) being erected towards the end of the run and one of the final steam locomotives to be built by the company. No. 45448 travels northward past the Lancashire County Hall, Preston, with an 'Illuminations' Special for Blackpool on 8th September 1962.

Above **ROTHERHAM MASBROUGH STATION**

BR Type 4 diesel D157 has probably developed an issue on 23rd August 1963 requiring the assistance of Stanier Class 5 no. 44871. The train is the 'Waverley', or 10.15 Edinburgh Waverley to St Pancras via Carlisle, which is seen at Rotherham Masbrough station from Coronation Bridge at the south end.

Opposite above **PRESTON**

Just south of Preston at Skew Bridge (now perhaps identified as Lower Penwortham) Stanier Class 5 no. 45184 is on the Up Slow line with a Class H freight train on 20th June 1957. Prior to ordering 227 Class 5s from Armstrong Whitworth & Co. the LMSR had 100 of the class erected by the company between April and December 1935, with no. 45184 appearing in September. This batch was fitted with the new boiler featuring a 21-element superheater, but retaining a straight firebox throatplate, smokebox-mounted regulator and top-feed on the second boiler ring. In some instances these boilers would later be replaced by the 24-element boiler, but no. 45184 has stuck to the original type. The locomotive was withdrawn in September 1965.

Opposite below **RADLETT STATION**

North of Radlett station — on the Midland main line south of St Albans — Fowler 3P Class 2-6-4T no. 40022 ambles along the Down Slow line with the 17.20 local train from St Pancras to St Albans. Constructed at Derby Works in January 1931, the locomotive was one of thirty 3Ps to be built during the year and fitted with condensing apparatus for working in the tunnels of the Metropolitan Widened Lines in London. Interestingly, no. 40022 was the last of the class to be condemned in December 1962 after the process of eliminating them had begun three years earlier.

Above **ROTHERHAM CANKLOW**

Rotherham Main Colliery stands in the barren background of this picture, taken on 10th April 1949. The pit was established by Sheffield steel firm John Brown & Co. in 1890 and was working four seams by the mid-1890s. The colliery and the steel works were both served by the MR, later LMSR, and there were large yards for assembling trains to convey the respective products. Johnson 1F 0-6-0T no. 1805 has been at work in one — likely Masbrough Sidings just to the north of the colliery — and is seen returning to Canklow shed.

Opposite above **ROTHERHAM CANKLOW SHED**

A mix of corporate identities are on display at Rotherham Canklow shed on Sunday, 10th April 1949. Six locomotives rest before being called back into action and they are, from left to right: three 0-6-0Ts; 2F no. 22965; 3F no. 43817; 4F no. 4128. The latter was built at Crewe Works during August 1925 and was in traffic until December 1962, spending all but the last month of BR service allocated to Canklow depot. 3F no. 43817 was visiting from Toton shed and after two years at Saltley from 1953 to 1955 the engine was withdrawn. No. 22965 was erected by Beyer Peacock & Co. in March 1876 as no. 1197, becoming no. 2965 in 1907 and another '2' was added in 1934. Interestingly, the locomotive is not recorded as having the BR number (58147) applied, even though the locomotive remained in traffic until the end of 1952 — being allocated to Canklow from 1948 (at least) until this time.

Opposite below **ROTHERHAM CANKLOW SHED**

Canklow engine shed was a late addition beside the ex-NMR line south-west of Rotherham. The facilities appeared in 1900 and consisted of a square roundhouse with 55 ft turntable and ramped coal stage just to the north. The allocation was of 40 engines for shunting and freight work, later rising to over 70 at Nationalisation. Johnson 2F (MR 1698) Class 0-6-0 no. 58238 was one resident at this time, being pictured there slightly later on 10th April 1949. The locomotive had been constructed at Derby Works in December 1886 as no. 1764 and received the BR number in mid-1948. Creditably, no. 58238 managed to survive (at Canklow) until late 1957; in the following year the shed was taken over by the ER. Canklow closed to steam in October 1965 and has since been demolished.

Above ROYSTON & NOTTON STATION

Royston & Notton station was opened by the NMR on 6th April 1841 and was rebuilt to the south of the original site when line improvements were made at the turn of the century; this station remained open until 1st January 1968. Fowler 4F no. 44538 is pictured at the north end of the station on 24th July 1951 with a train of coal wagons; in the background is Monckton Main Colliery and there were extensive sidings on the east side of the line to the south of the station for Carlton Main Colliery.

Opposite above ROYSTON & NOTTON STATION

After entering service in November 1927 (as no. 13094), Hughes 'Crab' Class 2-6-0 no. 42794 was first allocated to Grimesthorpe before quickly switching to Derby and remained there for the next two years. In March 1930 no. 42794 returned to Grimesthorpe until 1944, first being loaned to Agecroft, then reallocated to Toton, Wellingborough and Nottingham in quick succession, finally settling at Cricklewood between 1947 and 1954. The engine had worked quite a distance from there when pictured on the Up Fast line at Royston & Notton station on 24th July 1951 with a Class D freight; on the right is Fowler 4F no. 44374. No. 42794 returned to Grimesthorpe in November 1954 and moved away for the final time in July 1961, being housed at Wigan until condemned in November 1963.

Opposite below ROYSTON SHED

Located just to the south of Royston & Notton station on the east side of the ex-North Midland Railway line, Royston shed was a relatively new facility, opened by the LMSR in 1932. The building was large with 10 roads and had a coaling plant, but no turntable — a turning triangle was installed instead; on a contemporary map a turntable is visible a short distance to the south and connected to Carlton North Sidings which could be the reason for the omission. Johnson 2228 Class 0-4-4T locomotive no. 1368 is seen in the shed yard on 10th April 1949 and was a resident at Royston over two periods under BR before withdrawn in October 1958. The engine has been fitted for auto-train working, which in this instance meant the local Cudworth to Barnsley train.

Above **RUGBY SHED**

Beames 7F (LNWR G2) Class 0-8-0 no. 49431 was erected at Crewe Works in July 1922 and remained in service for another 40 years. No. 49431 was allocated to Rugby (where pictured) from Bescot in late 1948 and remained at the depot until November 1955 when switching to Market Harborough. The engine would later move on to Coventry, Nuneaton and Wigan Springs Branch depots before condemned.

Opposite above **RUGBY SHED**

View across the yard to Rugby shed on Sunday, 15th March 1953. The depot was one of the largest and busiest for the LNWR, but was downsized in the 1950s. The first shed on this site opened in 1876 on the north side of Rugby station and only 10 years later a second building was erected adjoining the north wall. The latter shed dominates this picture, with the earlier building, which was rebuilt in 1955, mainly off to the left. Standing outside, from left to right are: Stanier Class 5 no. 45000; Webb Class B 0-8-0 no. 48915, rebuilt with G2A specifications; Fowler 3F Class 0-6-0T no. 47379; Stanier Class 8F no. 48085; Beames G2 Class 0-8-0 no. 49452; Beames G2 Class 0-8-0 no. 49447. The 1886 shed was closed in 1960 and the 1876 building followed five years later, but was reused for a time before final closure.

Opposite below **RUGELEY TRENT VALLEY STATION**

The Trent Valley Railway was an independent undertaking with the aim of providing a diversion away from the congested lines in Birmingham. The route left the main line south of Stafford and went via Lichfield and Nuneaton to Rugby. One of several stations opened with the line on 15th September 1847 was Rugeley, which was renamed Rugeley Trent Valley in June 1870. About a decade before this time, the station had been connected with Birmingham by the South Staffordshire Railway line from Walsall. Rushing northward through the station on 9th April 1958 is Stanier 'Jubilee' Class no. 45643 *Rodney*, which is at the head of a fully-fitted freight. Although passenger services to Birmingham and the 'Trent Valley' portion of the name were dropped in the 1960s, both were restored in the 1990s.

Above **SALFORD STATION**

Stanier 'Jubilee' Class no. 45559 *British Columbia* looks underworked with this short train forming the 16.05 express from Manchester Exchange to Liverpool Lime Street. The engine was one of the early arrivals from the NBLC's Hyde Park Works, being ready for traffic in early July 1934. At this time the engine was decorated in the LMSR's express passenger locomotive livery of Crimson Lake with yellow and black lining, but during the war this became plain black and following the conflict lining was applied to some, no. 45559 being so decorated in late 1948. From November 1952 *British Columbia* had BR green with orange and black lining applied and this remained in use (under the many layers of dirt and grime) until the engine was withdrawn in July 1968.

Opposite above **RUGELEY TRENT VALLEY STATION**

Stanier Class 5 no. 45045 pilots 'Patriot' Class no. 45514 *Holyhead* through Rugeley Trent Valley station with the 12.50 Bangor to London Euston express on 9th April 1958. No. 45045 was constructed at Vulcan Foundry in October 1934 as part of an early order for 50 and these were fitted with the 14-element domeless boiler. The locomotive would receive an improved boiler at the first general repair and has subsequently been equipped with a domed boiler with sloping firebox throatplate; this type was carried until withdrawn in October 1966. No. 45045 was allocated to Crewe South when pictured, while no. 45514 was a Camden resident.

Opposite below **SALFORD STATION**

View east from the Up platform at Salford station as Stanier Class 5 no. 44864 builds up speed after departing from Manchester Victoria station with the 16.30 express to Llandudno on 9th June 1959. The locomotive was erected at Crewe Works in January 1945 and was later allocated to Holyhead from 1949 until late 1956 when transferred to Llandudno. No. 44864 had over a year and a half left there before moving on to Speke Junction and, following several further reallocations, was condemned in May 1968.

Above **SALWICK STATION**

Salwick station was opened by the Preston & Wyre Joint Railway in late 1840, some months after the opening of the line between Preston and the coast. The station was closed in May 1938, only to be reopened two years later for workers in a factory connected with the war effort, then in 1942 for the general public. These two engines have no intention of stopping at Salwick on 1st August 1959 and are working hard with their respective expresses. Hughes 'Crab' no. 42775 is on the left and on the right is Stanier Class 5 no. 45428, which has the 09.35 from Blackpool North to Nottingham.

Opposite above **SALFORD STATION**

The Manchester, Bolton & Bury Canal Co. promoted a scheme for a railway line to shadow the route of the canal in the early 1830s. Construction began in 1833, but difficulties were encountered and the project limped to completion in 1838. The southern terminus of the line was Salford station, but five years later a connection was formed with Manchester Victoria station, which opened in 1844. Soon after the line was taken over by the Manchester & Leeds Railway and in turn the Lancashire & Yorkshire Railway. On 9th June 1959 Stanier 2-6-4T no. 42456 has been pictured at Salford station coupled with the 17.05 Manchester Exchange to Wigan local. The engine was erected at Derby Works in October 1936 and was in service until April 1965. From 1994 Salford station has been renamed Salford Central to distinguish the facility from others in the area.

Opposite below **SALWICK STATION**

The passengers on these racing trains had little chance to see the well-tended flower arrangements on the station platform at Salwick on 1st August 1959. Having a slight edge on the left is Stanier Class 5 no. 44971, but Thompson B1 Class 4-6-0 no. 61281, which possessed a slightly greater tractive effort, still had a chance of taking the glory for the LNER. Both engines headed expresses bound for Blackpool and, while no. 44971's origin is unknown (perhaps the Chester area being allocated to Mold Junction at the time), no. 61281's train had started at Hull. Ben Brooksbank notes that on this particular day during his time at the station — just over four hours — 142 expresses passed by with only three having diesel locomotives at their head.

Above **SETTLE JUNCTION**

Settle Junction was where the 'Little' North Western Railway line diverged west to Lancaster, Morecambe and Heysham and the Ingleton branch between Clapham and Tebay. Stanier Class 8F no. 48758 will not take that route, but the Settle to Carlisle line as far as Kirkby Thore where this train of empty gypsum wagons will be refilled on 22nd September 1962. No. 48758 was constructed at Doncaster Works in December 1945 as O6 Class no. 3185 (later no. 3553) and was later returned to the LMSR in September 1947. In 1952 the engine took up residence at Carlisle Kingmoor shed and remained there until July 1964 when transferred to Newton Heath. Withdrawal from there occurred in December 1967.

Opposite above **SALWICK STATION**

The 10.20 from Fleetwood to Manchester passes through Salwick station on 1st August 1959 behind Hughes 'Crab' Class no. 42844; another express is already approaching in the distance. The locomotive was erected at Horwich Works in October 1930 and spent much of the next 35 years working in and around the north west. No. 42844's longest allocation was between June 1950 and June 1964 at Fleetwood depot.

Opposite below **SETTLE JUNCTION**

Another Stanier 'Jubilee' Class 4-6-0 has charge of a short express; in this instance no. 45675 *Hardy* is pictured with the 12.43 from Bradford Forster Square to Morecambe Promenade station at Settle Junction on 22nd September 1962. With the 'Jubilee' Class entering service at the time of George V's Silver Jubilee, the decision was taken to name the class in celebration of this event, with the British Empire and the Navy the main subjects, but with others making up the numbers. Although not immediately recognisable to the layman, *Hardy* was bestowed upon the engine in March 1937 in recognition of Sir Thomas Hardy (1769-1839) who was active in the Royal Navy during the French Revolutionary Wars and the Napoleonic Wars. He served under Nelson several times and was the Flag Captain on HMS Victory at the Battle of Trafalgar, being with Nelson when the latter was shot during the battle and shortly before he died; he was the subject of the famous quote "Kiss me, Hardy."

Above **SHEFFIELD MIDLAND STATION**

The North Midland Railway only skirted along the eastern edge of Sheffield thanks to George Stephenson, who wanted to keep adverse gradients on the line to a minimum. A connection between the city and the NMR was made via the Sheffield & Rotherham Railway and this remained the case for decades subsequently. By the 1860s this situation was deemed unacceptable by the MR and a new line was planned from Chesterfield to Sheffield. The people of Sheffield were not keen on this following the initial snub by the NMR, but Parliament gave approval and Sheffield Midland station opened on the east side of the city in 1870. This view has been taken there from platform 8 on 25th April 1950 and sees Class 5 no. 44665 on the through line and Stanier Class 3 2-6-2T no. 40181 on pilot duty.

Opposite **SCOUT GREEN**

The inhospitable fells and dales between Lancaster and Carlisle were not tackled by a railway company until the mid-1840s when the Lancaster & Carlisle Railway took up the challenge. Several of the day's most eminent engineers surveyed the route and Joseph Locke's proposal was accepted. The first sod was cut at Shap summit in mid-July 1844 and work progressed surprisingly quickly, being completed in under three years at a cost of over £1,000,000. Both climbs up to Shap summit were difficult, but the greater challenge was perhaps the southerly approach from Tebay. This consisted of (approx.) two miles at 1 in 146, then four miles at 1 in 75. The mid-way point was Scout Green and this is the location for these two pictures of a heavy freight train being dragged over the top on 7th October 1961; note the guard admiring the scenery. Leading is Stanier Class 5 no. 45380 and assisting at the rear is Fowler 2-6-4T no. 42424. The latter was a long-term resident of Tebay shed (1948-March 1963) but was later moved on to Stockport and was condemned there in September 1964. No. 45380 (built by Armstrong Whitworth & Co. in July 1937) had a long association with Edge Hill shed during the 1950s, but had eight moves before withdrawn in March 1965; at the time of the photograph the engine was at Warrington Dallam.

Above SHOTTON STATION

View west (dating from 30th July 1966) on the Chester to Holyhead line at Shotton as Stanier Class 5 no. 44863 passes by with a relatively short train of oil tankers. The aforementioned route did not have a station to serve the town when ready for traffic in 1848 and not until some time after the opening of the Wrexham, Mold & Connah's Quay Railway in 1890 did the LNWR take action. Shotton station (just behind the bridge in the distance which carried the WM&CR line) was opened on 1st April 1907 and was connected to Connah's Quay and Shotton station to allow free movement of passengers. After Nationalisation the pair were renamed Shotton Low Level and Shotton High Level respectively. The former was closed in February 1966, only to be reopened in the early 1970s and both continue to serve the area.

Opposite above SHIREBROOK STATION

Shirebrook station was opened on the MR's Nottingham to Worksop line on 1st June 1875 and the facility subsequently remained open until 12th October 1964; for the last 13 years the title Shirebrook West was used to set the station apart from several others in the area. The station was resurrected in May 1998 as part of the Robin Hood line. On 17th June 1957 Fowler Class 2P 4-4-0 no. 40632 breaks the tranquillity as the engine hauls an Inspection Saloon northward. The spoil heap in the background belongs to Shirebrook Colliery.

Opposite below SHREWSBURY STATION

The boundaries of the British Railways' Regions often blurred as locomotives passed over them with inter-city expresses that followed pre-Nationalisation and pre-Grouping companies' lines. This was the case at Shrewsbury which was the focal point for several important LMR routes from Chester, Crewe, Birmingham, Wolverhampton and Stafford. The last mentioned is the destination for Stanier 'Jubilee' Class no. 45572 *Eire* on 29th June 1962, being attached to a local service. The locomotive was allocated to the ex-GWR/LMSR joint shed at Shrewsbury, taking a berth there between October 1961 and January 1964 when condemned.

Above **SILEBY**

BR Standard Class 9F 2-10-0 no. 92159 heads an Up mixed freight train past Humble Lane bridge, south of Sileby, Leicestershire, on 4th June 1962. The locomotive was added to BR stock from Crewe Works in November 1957 and allocated to Wellingborough, remaining there until 1964 (apart from a month at Cricklewood in late 1958). Rowsley, Kirkby-in-Ashfield, Newton Heath and Birkenhead were visited before withdrawn after a disappointingly short service life of under ten years.

Opposite above **SHREWSBURY STATION**

This scene — captured from platform 5 at Shrewsbury station on 29th June 1962 — features Stanier Class 5 no. 45298 and Stanier 4P Class 2-6-4T no. 42488. The former was constructed by Armstrong Whitworth & Co. in December 1937 and would go on to amass nearly 30 years of service. A good proportion of this was performed from Shrewsbury shed, where the engine was based from 1948 until 1964. No. 42488 was erected at Derby Works during April 1937 and was condemned for scrap in February 1965. The engine spent most of the 1950s allocated to Walsall shed, but by the time of this photograph several transfers had occurred and the locomotive was on the cusp of switching from Aston to Stafford. Shrewsbury station was built by the Shrewsbury & Chester Railway to the design of noted local architect T.W. Penson and opened on 14th October 1848.

Opposite below **SILEBY**

View south from Humble Lane (south of Sileby) bridge over the Midland main line between Loughborough and Leicester on 4th June 1962. Stanier 8F no. 48395 was one of seventy five erected at Horwich Works to an LMSR order between 1943 and 1945, entering traffic in May 1945. Some engines of this batch (including no. 48395) and other 8Fs constructed during this period were fitted with thicker frame plates — 1⅛ in. against 1¹/₁₆ in. beforehand and 1 in. originally — in order to reduce the instances of cracked frames. No. 48395 was mainly associated with Kirkby-in-Ashfield shed during the BR years, having started the period at Normanton and the engine had a spell at Toton during the middle of the 1950s. Withdrawal occurred from Edge Hill shed in September 1967 after six months there.

Above **SPRINGS BRANCH JUNCTION**

Springs Branch Junction, south of Wigan, was the location for two major divergences from the WCML. Heading westward was the line to St Helens and Liverpool and forging east was the line to Manchester. Stanier 8F no. 48340 is seen with an Up freight on 3rd May 1965, perhaps taking the junction to the east. When built at Horwich Works in January 1940, the locomotive was paired with a Stanier 4,000 gallon tender with a welded tank, but this has subsequently been swapped with a Fowler 3,500 gallon example. No. 48340 was one of the final steam locomotive withdrawals in early August 1968.

Opposite **SKIPTON STATION**

The 'Thames-Clyde Express' was inaugurated by the LMSR in 1927, running between Glasgow St Enoch and London St Pancras stations. The Up express left at 09.30 and the Down express at 10.00. Initially the timing was not taxing for the 'Jubilee' and 'Royal Scots' assigned to the service, given the generally difficult nature of the route, but before the war schedules for certain sections were tightened. These were relaxed during and after the conflict and never recovered, but an alteration was that of the start times, being 09.15 from Glasgow and 09.50 from St Pancras, and both took just over 10 hours. Still with some way to go from Skipton on a wet and gloomy day in mid-April 1961 is this Down train headed by BR Standard Class 'Britannia' Pacific no. 70044 *Earl Haig*.

Above **STAFFORD STATION**

Newport Road provides the vantage point for this view (taken looking north west) of Stafford station on 14th April 1960. Stanier Class 5 no. 45097 is seen just getting away from the Up Main platform with a relief express bound for Euston station. The engine was constructed at Vulcan Foundry in April 1935 and was an early recipient of a sloping throatplate boiler in March 1937, subsequently carrying this type until condemned in June 1966.

Opposite above **STAFFORD STATION**

Another scene at Stafford station captured from the same position as above. This was the third facility to be erected on the site when opened in 1862, following two from 1844 and 1837 — the original being installed by the Grand Junction Railway. Stafford was only two years away from being completely rebuilt for the electrification of the WCML, becoming a victim of the architectural style of the time. Here, Hughes 'Crab' no. 42931 heads a southbound fast freight.

Opposite below **STAFFORD STATION**

View to the south of Newport Road bridge as Stanier 'Jubilee' Class no. 45571 *South Africa* approaches on the Down Fast line with a Relief express. In the background is Stafford No. 4 signal box, on the right the extensive goods sidings and out of view on the left was the goods station; the pilot can be seen at work in the distance.

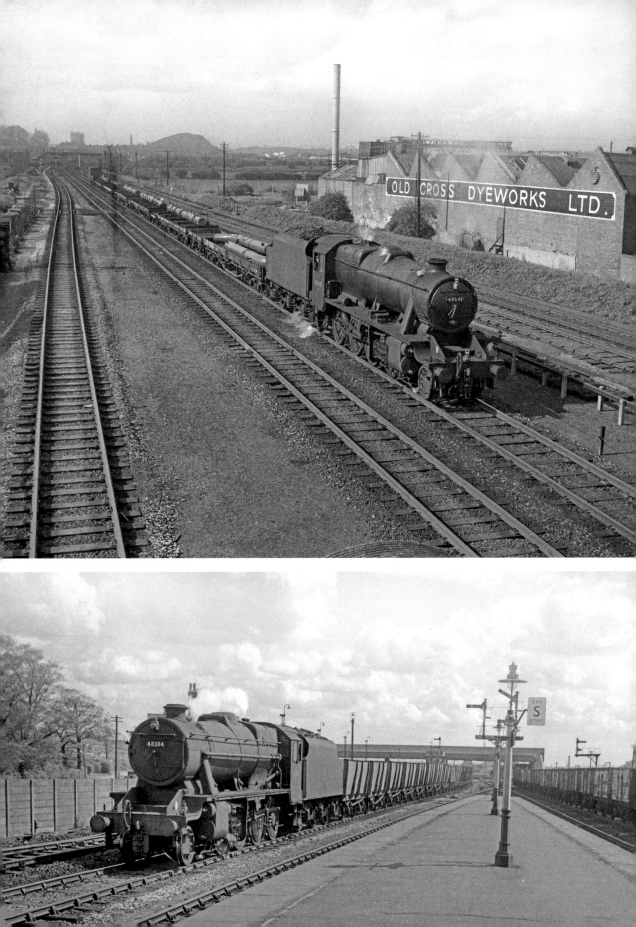

OLD CROSS DYEWORKS LTD.

·48641·

48384

Above STAVELEY WORKS

The Staveley Coal & Iron Company was formed near Chesterfield in the early 1860s as an ironworks, but later the concern turned into new fields, such as coal mining and manufacturing chemicals. As a result, materials and products had to be moved around the extensive site, which was located to the east of Staveley town. In the main the company leased locomotives from, first the MR, then LMSR and finally LMR for these tasks and they operated from Barrow Hill shed a short distance to the north west. Johnson 1F (MR 1377) Class 0-6-0T no. 41804 was one of four class members to serve the works and is seen near the junction with the ex-NMR line east of Whittington station on 23rd August 1963.

Opposite above STAPLEFORD & SANDIACRE STATION

A train of flat wagons (loaded with unidentified tubular objects) led by Stanier 8F no. 48641 approaches Stapleford & Sandiacre Station from the north on 17th May 1962. The locomotive was the second of Lot No. 168 to be erected at Brighton Works in October 1943 and was in traffic until November 1966. At Nationalisation no. 8641 was noted at Kirkby-in-Ashfield shed, but in early 1950 a move to Stourton occurred and the engine remained there until sent for scrap. Originally in the LMR, Stourton shed was subsequently taken into the ER and the shedcode changed from 20B to 55B in 1957; the latter is applied in this instance.

Opposite below STAPLEFORD & SANDIACRE STATION

The Erewash Valley line served many collieries and other industries, resulting in quite intensive freight traffic. In spite of the massive decline of these subsequently the line manages to survive for freight traffic and long-distance passenger services, with many of the local stations having disappeared in the 1960s. One was Stapleford & Sandiacre Station which ceased serving the local population in 1967 after 120 years. Another Stanier 8F is seen passing through with a freight train, but in this instance is travelling northward. From at least Nationalisation to February 1964 no. 48384 was based at Toton depot, which was a short distance to the south. Later, after several moves, no. 48384 was withdrawn from Rose Grove shed, Burnley, in May 1968.

Above **STOCKPORT CHEADLE HEATH**

The MR had to travel on 'foreign' metals to reach Manchester from New Mills at the end of the line from Ambergate, north of Derby. This, and the sharing of London Road station with the LNWR, resulted in the construction of a new route from New Mills via Hazel Grove and Heaton Mersey. The project was completed in July 1902 and one of the stations was Cheadle Heath for Stockport which was a short distance west of the town centre. On 28th July 1951 a Llandudno to Sheffield express approaches the station behind no. 44831, passing Cheadle Heath North signal box which controlled the junction of the MR line with the line to Cheadle and the Cheshire Lines Committee route to Glazebrook.

Opposite above **STAVELEY WORKS**

Johnson's 1377 Class was introduced in 1878 with 20 constructed at Derby Works and a steady stream followed through to 1891 (although there was a short break between 1886 and 1889). The final order for 20 was completed at Vulcan Foundry in 1892, at which time there were 185 locomotives to the design in traffic. No. 41804, which is seen again at Staveley Works, was erected at Derby in December 1890 as no. 889. The locomotive was later a long-term resident at Barrow Hill shed and managed to survive there until the depot closed in October 1965. Afterwards no. 41804 spent 14 months at Langwith Junction (a short distance away, north of Mansfield) before being condemned for scrap. One of the Barrow Hill contingent — no. 41708, which also made the trip to Langwith Junction — was preserved.

Opposite below **STOCKPORT STATION**

A fine array of LNWR signals controlled the approaches to the north end of Stockport station, being placed on the impressive Stockport Viaduct. This structure was completed by the Manchester & Birmingham Railway in 1840, requiring approx. 11,000,000 bricks which were laid in just under two years. A major upgrade of the viaduct was undertaken in the 1890s as two extra running lines were added, requiring extensions to the 27 arches. Fowler 3P Class 2-6-2T no. 40061 has just passed over with this local train from Oldham via Stalybridge on 31st July 1950.

Above **STOCKPORT STATION**

On the Up Through road — with a Palethorpe's sausage van on the next line — at Stockport station on 21st June 1957 is Stanier 'Jubilee' Class 4-6-0 no. 45578 *United Provinces*. Initially, the Manchester & Birmingham Railway only stretched between Manchester Travis Street and the north bank of the River Mersey at Stockport as the Stockport Viaduct (seen here in the background) was yet to be constructed. When this task was completed, a new station (sometimes known as Stockport Edgeley) was built at the southern end of the viaduct and the first station became of second importance, being renamed Heaton Norris.

Opposite above **STOCKPORT STATION**

WD 'Austerity' no. 90669 waits for a short freight train to clear the lines over Stockport Viaduct on 12th June 1957. This short delay has given the fireman the chance to assess the coal supply in the tender, which had a coal capacity of 9 tons and a 5,000-gallon water tank, and have a cigarette. The locomotive was built at Vulcan foundry in October 1944 and was subsequently in service until February 1966, being allocated to Newton Heath depot from the early 1950s to 1961.

Opposite below **STOCKPORT STATION**

Fowler 4F no. 44444 was unique in being the only BR locomotive to carry a number with five identical digits; several locomotives at Grouping and beforehand had numbers with four identical digits. However, when built at Crewe Works in December 1927, there was already an engine with no. 4444, which was Ivatt C1 Class Atlantic (previously GNR no. 1444) and another would receive the number before Nationalisation. This was Robinson J11 no. 5016 and no. 4444 was received under Thompson's renumbering scheme of 1946. No. 44444 is pictured shunting wagons at the south end of Stockport station on 31st July 1950.

Above **STOKE STATION**

BR Standard Class 4 2-6-0 no. 76099 was the last steam locomotive constructed at Horwich Works in November 1957; from then until 1962 the engine was allocated to Glasgow Corkerhill shed. The engine was briefly at Ardrossan before withdrawn in June 1964, only to get a reprieve from the LMR and a move to Saltley depot. By early 1965 no. 76099 was at Stoke shed and is seen at the station on 4th May 1965 with a lengthy coal train. Withdrawal for the second and final time occurred in August 1966 while at Colwick.

Opposite above **STOKE HAMMOND**

The 16.35 Down Euston to Wolverhampton express approaches Newton Road bridge, Stoke Hammond, on 4th July 1959. The locomotive is Stanier Class 5 no. 45405 which was erected by Armstrong Whitworth in September 1937 and spent just short of 30 years in traffic, being condemned in August 1967. The engine was allocated to Bushbury shed, Wolverhampton, at the time of the photograph.

Opposite below **STOKE HAMMOND**

At Nationalisation LMSR CME H.G. Ivatt was engaged with improvements for Stanier's Class 5 design. These included changes to the boiler (the top feed moved further forward), the cylinders and motion (22 were fitted with British Caprotti motion), the axleboxes (roller bearings were used) and draughting (double chimney). There were certain problems with the British Caprotti arrangement and the final two locomotives — nos 44686 and 44687, which were also the last Class 5s — had an improved design fitted. No. 44686 is seen here at Stoke Hammond with an Up parcels train on 7th May 1960.

Above **STONEYFORD**

An Up empty mineral train passes through Stoneyford on the Erewash Valley line between Codnor Park and Langley Mill on 12th July 1963. The locomotive is BR Standard Class 9F 2-10-0 no. 92117 which was erected at Crewe Works in December 1956 and in service until December 1967.

Opposite above **STOKE STATION**

The pottery producing areas of Staffordshire were bypassed when the Grand Junction Railway line was laid in the mid-1830s. Local businessmen were eager to rectify this oversight and in the early 1840s several schemes were brought under the direction of the North Staffordshire Railway. The main route was between the LNWR line north of Norton Bridge, near Stafford, to Stone, Stoke, Kidsgrove, Congleton and Macclesfield. Completed in April 1848, a temporary station served Stoke until replaced in October by the present station, which was renamed Stoke-on-Trent just before city status was granted in 1925. The station subsequently became the hub for all the company's lines in the area. Here, on 4th May 1965, Stanier 8F no. 48452 passes through with a short Up freight, whilst a local service is seen on the left with Stanier 2-6-4T no. 42665; both were allocated to Stoke shed at this time.

Opposite below **STOKE SHED**

Two locomotive sheds were constructed at Stoke to house the NSR's motive power. The first was a roundhouse which was built in 1852 on the west side of the main line and the second was a six-track straight shed almost directly opposite on the east side of the running lines in 1872. The latter is the location for this picture — taken on 1st October 1966 — and shows Fowler 3F 0-6-0T no. 47273, which is on the cusp of being condemned, as well as BR Standard Class 4 4-6-0 no. 75062 (withdrawn in February 1968). Being off the main line, 4-6-0s were not kept in numbers at Stoke, whereas 0-6-0s, 0-6-0Ts, and 2-6-4Ts dominated for local work. The sheds closed to steam in 1967 and were later demolished.

Above STONEYFORD

No. 92126 works hard with a fully laden iron ore train at Stoneyford and is progressing northward along the two miles at 1 in 258 between Langley Mill and Codnor Park. The locomotive is also under a temporary speed restriction due to mining subsidence and this is displayed by the signal on the right. No. 92126 was working from Wellingborough shed (the engine's home from new in March 1957) when pictured on 12th July 1963, but would move to Kettering in 1964 and Warrington in 1965, being condemned there in August 1967.

Opposite above STONEYFORD JUNCTION

Stoneyford Junction signal box is passed by BR Standard Class 5 no. 73137 — a Caprotti-fitted engine — which has charge of a southbound goods train. The box's name is slightly misleading as a connection was not formed with another route, but there was perhaps access to the mineral line from Pollington Colliery to the north east. The main task of the box appears to have been controlling sidings adjacent to the main line.

Opposite below STONEYFORD

Fairburn Class 4P 2-6-4T no. 42185 appears underemployed with this short local parcels train at Stoneyford. The engine was erected at Derby Works in February 1949 and when pictured on 12th July 1963 had just under a year left in traffic; no. 42185 spent this entire period allocated to Nottingham shed.

Above **STONEYFORD**

Another locomotive working hard at Stoneyford is Fowler 4F Class 0-6-0 no. 44054, which has a loose-coupled freight train. Constructed at Derby Works in May 1925, the engine was withdrawn from Westhouses shed in December 1964 after only two months there. Prior to this allocation, no. 44054 was based at Hasland depot, south of Chesterfield, from at least Nationalisation.

Opposite above **TAMWORTH HIGH LEVEL STATION**

Tamworth was first reached by the Birmingham & Derby Junction Railway in mid-1839. Then, by the end of the following decade, the Trent Valley Railway had been completed, which also passed through the town. A new station to serve both lines was constructed at this time, with the High Level station (this designation only being used from 1924) serving the ex-B&DJR and the Low Level station the TVR, operated by the LNWR. Johnson 3F Class 0-6-0 no. 43709 is seen at the High Level station with a Down coal train on 20th December 1961. The station is in the midst of reconstruction as part of the WCML electrification scheme.

Opposite below **TEBAY STATION**

Tebay station closed in mid-1968 and has since been demolished, but was once a relatively important railway centre for the area. Opened by the Lancaster & Carlisle Railway in late 1846, Tebay served the village and was a staging point for locomotives about to tackle Shap bank. In the early 1860s Tebay became the terminus for the South Durham & Lancashire Junction Railway from Bishop Auckland and Barnard Castle, in addition to the branch line from Ingleton. Here, 'Royal Scot' no. 46127 *The Old Contemptibles* heads the 09.05 from Crewe to Perth on 7th October 1961.

Above **UTTOXETER STATION**

View west at Uttoxeter station on 13th June 1959 as Fairburn 2-6-4T no. 42184 arrives with a local freight train on the ex-North Staffordshire Railway line from Stoke.

Opposite above **TIBSHELF SIDINGS**

The MR/LMSR upgraded the boilers of the Standard Goods Class several times during the lifetime of the locomotives. When built by Neilson & Co. in July 1890, Johnson 1798 Class 0-6-0 no. 1908 was fitted with the standard 4 ft 2 in. diameter boiler with round-top firebox working at 150 lb per sq. in. Only 12 years later the engine received an upgraded B type boiler pressed to 160 lb per sq. in., then in 1920 the engine (as no. 3235) was fitted with a larger diameter G7 boiler working at 175 lb per sq. in. No. 43235 is seen approaching Tibshelf Sidings on the Erewash Valley line with an empties train on 13th June 1957.

Opposite below **TRENT STATION**

Trent station was the location for several junctions between the ex-Midland Counties Railway line from Leicester and the east and west spurs to Nottingham and Derby, as well as the Erewash Valley line. The station was mainly used to serve the various connections that could be made by passengers, although Long Eaton was not too far away to the north. Stanier 8F no. 48355 has just passed through Trent station with a train of iron ore empties on 24th April 1961 and has been given the Up Independent through line by Trent South signal box on the left.

Above **WARRINGTON BANK QUAY HIGH LEVEL STATION**

Another locomotive for the notebooks of these 'spotters' on Warrington Bank Quay High Level station's platform on 17th August 1963. Stanier Class 5 no. 45313 has the 06.20 semi-fast from Carlisle to Crewe. In the background is the Bank Quay soap works.

Opposite above **WARRINGTON BANK QUAY LOW LEVEL STATION**

Warrington Bank Quay Low Level station was built following the connection of two independent railway lines to the town which opened during 1853. Completed first was the St Helens & Runcorn Gap Railway's branch from Widnes and this originally terminated at Warrington White Cross station. Before the end of the year the Warrington & Altrincham Junction Railway was operational from the Manchester, South Junction & Altrincham Railway at Timperley to Warrington Wilderspool station. These temporary stations were replaced in 1854 when Warrington Arpley station was opened, but thoughts soon turned to a joint station with the WCML, which the line passed under, and this was completed in 1868, officially being called Warrington Bank Quay. Ivatt Class 2MT 2-6-2T no. 41211 is pictured with a local train at the Low Level station (the High Level is seen in the background) on 8th September 1962.

Opposite below **WARRINGTON BANK QUAY HIGH LEVEL STATION**

On 17th August 1963 Fowler Class 3F 0-6-0T no. 47531 approaches the south end of Warrington Bank Quay High Level station with a goods train which is being marshalled, perhaps between the extensive Arpley Extension Sidings and Bank Quay Goods Station.

Above WARRINGTON BANK QUAY HIGH LEVEL STATION

Two Stanier Class 5 4-6-0s head the 16.30 Manchester Victoria to Llandudno express at Warrington Bank Quay High Level station on 8th September 1962. Leading is no. 44802, whilst the train engine is no. 45441. The former was a product of Derby Works in June 1944 and spent most of the 1950s at work from Sheffield Grimesthorpe shed before moving to Holyhead in 1958, remaining there until the end of 1962. No. 45441 was erected by Armstrong Whitworth in December 1937 and in the early 1950s was allocated to Rugby. In the second half of the decade the engine toured various sheds in the north west but settled at Holyhead in mid-1957, lasting there until late 1962. The pair would take the ex-Birkenhead, Lancashire & Cheshire Railway line which ran from just south of the town to Chester and then the North Wales Coast line. Warrington No. 2 signal box (in the background, located at the north end of the station) dated from just before Grouping and would be removed with the opening of Warrington power signal box in the early 1970s.

Opposite above WATFORD JUNCTION STATION

The MR's last group of 50 new 0-4-4T locomotives for local passenger work was produced between 1895 and 1900 at Dübs & Co. (40) and Derby Works (10). In the early 1930s Derby Drawing Office was in the midst of designing a larger version of these earlier 0-4-4T, but following Stanier's arrival only 10 were erected. No. 41909 was the final engine to be constructed at Derby Works in January 1933 as no. 6409. The class had larger diameter coupled wheels and boiler, which was pressed to a slightly higher pressure. No. 41909 is seen here at Watford Junction station's St Albans Branch platform on 2nd October 1948. The engine was employed on the route until August 1955 and was later transferred to Warwick and Rugby before being withdrawn in November 1959.

Opposite below WATH ROAD

Stanier Class 5 no. 45404 passes by on the ex-NMR line at Wath Road (west of Mexborough) with a train of empty stock on 23rd August 1963. The Barnsley to Doncaster line passed underneath at this point and the Swinton to Knottingley line also diverged from the NMR line at Wath Road Junction.

Above **WELLINGBOROUGH LONDON ROAD STATION**

The London & Birmingham Railway expanded by building a line from Northampton to Peterborough via Wellingborough and Wansford and this opened in 1845. Fowler 4F no. 44215 is seen at Wellingborough London Road station on 18th August 1962 with the 16.00 local service from Peterborough East to Northampton.

Opposite above **WATH ROAD JUNCTION**

Travelling southward on the ex-NMR line at Wath Road Junction is Johnson 3F (MR 1798) Class no. 43233 which is coupled to a long coke train made up of standard and high capacity 20-ton wagons. The locomotive was one of fifty constructed by Neilson & Co. between February 1890 and August 1891, appearing in service in May 1890 as no. 1906. Fifteen years later the engine received received an H-type boiler, then at the dawn of Grouping a G7 boiler was fitted. No. 43233 is pictured on 28th April 1950 (the BR number was recently applied, but with LMSR-style numerals) and at this time was allocated to Royston shed; the engine would remain there until condemned in October 1959.

Opposite below **WEAVER JUNCTION**

Stanier Class 5 no. 44816 speeds towards Weaver Junction (on the WCML north of Acton Bridge) which was where the line to Liverpool diverged from that to Warrington, Wigan and the north. The engine is seen with the 17.20 relief express from Birmingham New Street to Liverpool Lime Street on 23rd April 1962.

Above **WIDNES SHED**

Widnes shed was built by the LNWR in the midst of the network of lines weaving their way past the many factories on the north bank of the River Mersey. The first building was only modest but in the late 1880s a large six-track shed was erected and remained in use until April 1964. Only two years before that time, two Stanier 2-6-2Ts (no. 40134 and no. 40143) stand withdrawn on lines to the south of the depot, whilst an Ivatt 2-6-2T is still in steam outside the shed.

Opposite above **WESTHOUSES & BLACKWELL STATION**

A station was built at Westhouses — on the Erewash Valley line north of Alfreton — with the route in the early 1860s, but the area was decidedly rural at this time and the station was soon closed. However, in 1881 the facility was resurrected, this time as Westhouses & Blackwell, perhaps due to an increase in employment at Blackwell Colliery — located a short distance away from the line and served by a branch. In 1890 an engine shed was erected just off the triangular junction, thus providing more employment; Tibshelf sidings were also sited just to the north. Fowler 4F no. 44070 travels on the Up Slow line just south of the station with a mixed freight train on 13th June 1957. Westhouses & Blackwell closed for the final time on 2nd January 1967; the engine shed survived until the late 1980s.

Opposite below **WHATSTANDWELL STATION**

Whatstandwell was the first station on the Derwent Valley line north of Ambergate Junction on the Midland main line. Originally, the station was located on the north side of the short tunnel (150 yards) seen in the background when built in 1849, but was resited on the south side in 1894 and continues to serve the local area. Stanier 8F no. 48547 passes through the station with a short Up freight on 23rd June 1961. The engine was one of thirty constructed to an order of the Railway Executive Committee at Darlington Works and entered traffic in March 1945. Chesterfield had no. 48547 on the roster at the time of the photograph and would until 1964. In July the locomotive transferred to Bolton and was withdrawn from there in March 1967.

Above WOLVERTON CARRIAGE WORKS

Once the largest carriage works in Great Britain, Wolverton subsequently suffered from the demise of the manufacturing industries, but thankfully remains open at present albeit with the strong possibility of closure for redevelopment.. On 10th October 1954 three of the four works shunters have been pictured near the old Royal Train shed at the works' southern extremity. All — nos 3, 6 and 7 — belonged to the once numerous LNWR Special Tank Class and, with classmate no. 8 *Earlstown* also at the works, made up the majority of the survivors at Nationalisation; the other was employed at Crewe Works.

Opposite above WIDNES

Widnes was only a rural area on the north bank of the River Mersey when the St Helens & Runcorn Gap Railway was built in the early 1830s. Following the opening of the line, which had the first rail to ship dock at Widnes, the area was soon seen as being ripe for industrialisation and a chemical works was founded. Widnes was later connected to Garston and Warrington by the SH&RGR, which was subsequently taken over by the LNWR. The Cheshire Lines Committee main route from Manchester to Liverpool bypassed the town to the north in 1873, but a branch was laid by the GCR and MR by the end of the decade. Ivatt Class 2MT 2-6-2T no. 41237 is seen with a short train for Spike Island sidings on the SH&RGR line to the east of Widnes South station, passing the Muspratt Chemical Works (James Muspratt was an original shareholder in the SH&RGR) on 16th April 1962. The line on the left went past the engine shed to connect with the deviation line built by the LNWR, which is seen crossing over on the bridge in the background; just beyond this the CLC also traversed the SH&RGR route.

Opposite below WIGAN NORTH WESTERN GOODS STATION

BR Standard Class 2 2-6-0 no. 78062 has been relegated to humble shunting duties at Wigan North Western goods station on 20th June 1957. The engine was quite young, having been completed at Darlington Works the previous October and was allocated to Wigan Central shed from this time to 1964. Fleetingly based at Wigan Springs Branch depot, no. 78062 spent a year at Nottingham and Toton to May 1965 when transferred to Gorton. The locomotive remained in the area until late 1966 and was condemned at Bolton during May 1967.

BIBLIOGRAPHY

Baker, Allan C. *The Book of the Coronation Pacifics Mk2*. 2010.

Christiansen, R. *Rail Centres: Crewe*. 2007.

Ellaway, K. J. *The Great British Railway Station: Euston*. 1994.

Griffiths, Roger and Paul Smith. *The Directory of British Engine Sheds and Principal Locomotive Servicing Points: Volume 1*. 1999.

Griffiths, Roger and Paul Smith. *The Directory of British Engine Sheds and Principal Locomotive Servicing Points: Volume 2*. 1999.

Haresnape, Brian. *Fowler Locomotives: A Pictorial History*. 1997.

Haresnape, Brian. *Stanier Locomotives: A Pictorial History*. 1974.

Hawkins, Chris and George Reeve. *LMS Engine Sheds Volume Two: The Midland Railway*. 1981.

Hooper, J. *The WD Austerity 2-8-0: The BR Record*. 2010.

Hunt, David, Fred James and Bob Essery with John Jennison and David Clarke. *LMS Locomotive Profiles No. 5: The Mixed Traffic Class 5s – Nos. 5000-5224*. 2003.

Hunt, David, Fred James and Bob Essery with John Jennison and David Clarke. *LMS Locomotive Profiles No. 6: The Mixed Traffic Class 5s – Nos. 5225-5499 and 4658-4999*. 2004.

Hunt, David, Fred James, John Jennison and Bob Essery. *LMS Locomotive Profiles No. 7: The Mixed Traffic Class 5s – Caprotti Valve Gear Engines*. 2006.

Hunt, David, John Jennison, Fred James and Bob Essery. *LMS Locomotive Profiles No. 8: The Class 8F 2-8-0s*. 2005.

Radford, Brian. *Rail Centres: Derby*. 2007.

Quick, Michael. *Railway Passenger Stations in Great Britain: A Chronology*. 2009.

RCTS. *British Railways Standard Steam Locomotives Volume 1: Background to Standardisation and the Pacific Classes*. 1994.

RCTS. *British Railways Standard Steam Locomotives Volume 2: The 4-6-0 and 2-6-0 Classes*. 2003.

RCTS *British Railways Standard Steam Locomotives Volume 3: The Tank Engine Classes*. 2007.

RCTS. *British Railways Standard Steam Locomotives Volume 4: The 9F 2-10-0 Class*. 2008.

Sixsmith, Ian. *The Book of the Ivatt 4MTs; LM Class 4 2-6-0s*. 2012.

Sixsmith, Ian. *The Book of the Royal Scots*. 2008.

Summerson, Stephen. *Midland Railway Locomotives: Volume 4*. 2005.

Townsin, Ray. *The Jubilee 4-6-0s*. 2006.

Walmsley, Tony. *Shed by Shed Part One: London Midland*. 2010.

Young, John and David Tyreman. *The Hughes and Stanier 2-6-0s*. 2009.

Also available from Great Northern by Peter Tuffrey

The Last Days of Scottish Steam

The Last Years of Yorkshire Steam

The Golden Age of Yorkshire Railways

Gresley's A3s

Peppercorn's Pacifics

visit *www.greatnorthernbooks.co.uk* for details.